WHAT IF…. you took a step?

This book is dedicated to my late wife Dorothea, who made it possible to get this whole thing started. Also to my son Thomas and my daughter Kristina.

And I'd be remiss if I didn't mention friend and board member Linda Shaul, who has been patient with me and has edited it.

INTRODUCTION

This book is written in hopes of inspiring and encouraging others. It was written by a pizza guy who fished a lot. I had a very checkered past, including drugs from an early age, arrests and jail times, etc. God has been able to use this guy in ways that are way beyond imagination.

I am reminded often of the story that my spiritual father used to tell. When Jesus was headed to Jerusalem on the donkey and all the people were praising Jesus and throwing their clothes and palm leaves to make a path, the donkey would've been real foolish to think all that praise was for him. And there's another word in

3

some versions of the Bible for donkey.... so please let this "donkey" write what it was like, what happened and what it's like today. There are lessons I learned from successes, and lessons I learned from my failures. Or best said, lessons I'm learning.

Reading this over I realize I use the word "I" what may seem like way too often. I don't mean it to be written about me. Yes it is about my experiences, my strength and my hope. It is about lessons I've learned and am learning. I personalize it so as not to impugn any of this on you the reader. But may I suggest that when you read it, you might look for similarities rather than differences. I bet many of you, if not most of you, did not have the checkered past I did and also did not have to learn the same lessons. However may I ask that you look for similarities? I hope you find strength and encouragement to take the next step in your own journeys. Or perhaps it might help you to get an understanding and some clarity in something you have been through or are going through now.

This book is not necessarily written for the strong, talented or gifted. Maybe so, but it is also written for the plain guy or girl, those that feel like they're uneducated, not good enough, too young, too old, not ready, or need to have more money. It's written for the beaten up and downtrodden. There's some things that some may think controversial, but I'm sharing my experience, my strength and my hope.

In writing this book I had no idea of how or where to start. The challenge seemed daunting. A friend suggested that I just speak into a phone or other device, ideas as they came to me. Sometimes I've had to pull over and make a note of what I'm thinking and there were times I've had a dream or just woke up and spent a few minutes talking into my phone about an idea that came to my mind. Sometimes it was just a thought that I needed to think about. More often than not, they were some lessons or things to practice and learn from.

So often I've questioned myself, "Who am I to write a book?" I certainly am no expert. I really am just a plain ol' guy that said yes to God. I came to a place that I'd rather be called a fool one more time than miss something that God had for me to do. I didn't know how to start or where to start from.

Many people have told me, "Robert you need to write a book!" I'm not sure this book is what they were talking about, but here it is.

My Story

I was the first born of an immigrant family who came from Russia after World War II. After Ellis Island they went to Boston, where my parents met. They got married and decided to move to California to get away from the winters. They moved to East Los Angeles. There were many families they knew from Russia, and it was a very tight knit community. I didn't learn to speak English until I went to kindergarten.

After 2nd grade we moved to Orange County. It was there that I began to feel different. It was the time of the cold war. Everybody was afraid of the spread of communism. I remember my third-grade teacher not liking me.

One day I came home telling my parents that my teacher doesn't like me. My parents went and met with her and when they came home they said, "Robert just sit quietly, don't ask questions, just sit there." It was at that time I felt prejudice, though I had no idea what it was.

I was overweight and didn't quite feel right or feel like I fit in. However, I struggled hard to fit in and I guess sort of did on the outside. But on the inside I still felt different, that I didn't measure up. Truth be told, even these days I often feel that way and need to use tools like saying, "just for today I'm good enough."

Around eighth grade I got into drugs. The goals I had in school were probably not the normal goals most have, like going to University. Instead, my goals were to be a drug dealer and live a life of criminal ways. The time was the late 60's early 70's. The Vietnam war was on, there was protest in the streets. Drugs and free love were the way, or at least the way I found. I got into very heavy drug use and selling of drugs. My future was bleak. It was the time of the Jesus movement. I remember in high school I kept wondering how come nobody invites me to get to know Jesus or invites me to church. I guess if I acted the way I did, I wouldn't invite me either.

My senior year, the predictions so many people had said, came true. After many arrests and a couple of drug treatment programs, my school had had enough. They told my probation officer that if I came within a mile of the school they wanted me arrested. I moved to a new city after another treatment and finished my high school degree going to a local community college and another high school.

At about 17 years old I got what I like to call "galvation". A girl that I became very fond of asked me to go to a prayer meeting. My motives were not pure to say the least.

Once we got to the prayer meeting she asked if I wanted to go get prayed for. I said, "sure, you bet baby!" I went up and the man prayed for me and had me go through a sinner's prayer. I said the words, but inside I was saying "No way, no way, no way." I did have an eye open making sure that my date was watching.

When the man finally let go of me, I took a few steps and had to lean on a nearby piano. I was about as sober as I could be at that time in my life, but I felt this surge or "rush," that felt like I had to stop walking, almost as if I was intoxicated. There was a strong feeling that I couldn't explain, even at 17 years old when we have all the answers.

At that point I said, "God if you're real, prove yourself to me." In the following weeks it seems like everything that I prayed for came through. At times I jokingly wished that I would've prayed for lottery numbers. I'm not even sure if there were lottery numbers then.

The problem was, I took the things of God and made them conform to my lifestyle. I never picked up a needle again, but I took things into my own hands. Yes, I continued to drink and drug, until the one day I walked into an Ed Cole meeting at a Christian Men's Network conference. It was in the morning and I had just been outside during the break wanting to smoke marijuana. However, for some reason I put it out and just didn't feel like it.

I came in a minute or two late for the start of the meeting and Dr. Cole had this chuckle. He looked out upon everybody and said, "We're all men here (forgive me ladies), how many of you understand that when a man walks with one leg on one side of the fence and one on the other and he falls down, it's going to hurt?" He was preaching from the Bible, in the book of James, where it says a double minded man is unstable in all his ways. But Dr. Cole said it in a way that I could understand. I got the message.

I wish I could say I walked out and never drank or drugged again. That wasn't the case for me. However, later that weekend Dr. Cole also shared that when we pray for wisdom, God will give us a strategy and when we keep the strategy we get the victory and go from victory to victory.

Within the year I went into treatment again and found a strategy that has kept me sober to the writing of this book over 33 years. What I learned was a game plan to live my life, to work and move forward to be more Christlike. To actually work to conform my lifestyle to Christlikeness. I fall way short, nonetheless, God has been able to use me to lead this organization called Giving It Back To Kids since April 2002.

I'm sure this book, or at least parts of it, you may or probably do disagree with, possibly even get upset with things I wrote. Part of me smiles if it upsets you. Way too often I've heard something or read something that upset me or even angered me. There's been books that I'd want to throw against a wall, but later after some more thought, realized there was truth for me to learn or make life changes.

Read this book much like I eat watermelon. I love watermelon but I spit out the seeds, the part that I don't like. Take what you like, disregard the rest or maybe even better, save it for another time. Those may just be the "seeds" for future growth.

Honestly I hope parts of it will make you feel uncomfortable, make you take a look and see what you could do in your life to transform others' lives. One of my favorite quotes is from Steve Jobs of Apple. At one of his meetings he looked out at his team and said, "Go dent the universe."

Puffed Up Versus Built Up

When I began to write this book I wrote lessons I learned and lessons I learned from my failures. I felt uncomfortable, or as I wrote in another place, I thought, "Who am I to say I learned this stuff?" As I think back and think about it, I recognize what I thought I learned. And today as I'm looking at it I see that maybe I was feeling puffed up and not built up. That I at times, may have been speaking more from head knowledge, rather than really being able to say, "I learned."

My hope in writing this book is to share my experience, that others might find moments of clarity. I'm sure at times there will be many who will think and say, "Well of course, who doesn't know that? Didn't everyone learn this when you were growing up?" Truth is no, I did not and I know today I am not alone. There are many who have yet to grow up like me.

Something happened in the writing of this book. It seems in writing of the things I kept saying I've learned, scene after scene would come up, challenging me in these areas that I "thought I learned." I came to the realization I'm still learning and I wish I could say I have this stuff down, but I don't. I guess if anything I

11

have become aware of, it has been moments of clarity when I begin to see some things in my life of leadership and the leading of this organization. I hope as you read this there might be at least one or two nuggets that will give you some things to think about. I guess for me it might be best said, "progress rather than perfection."

Learning Under Dr. Cole and Others

There is an importance of placing yourself in positions to be mentored. For years I'd hear others speak of a calling and ministry but would think, where's mine? Oh sure one could say, "You have helped and are helping so many already." But in my "gut" I felt there was to be more. There was a yearning to make a difference. What I did was stay in the process. I learned and most importantly, submitted myself to others like Dr. Cole.

I served setting up tables or selling books. At some places I cleaned coffee cups or set up and took down chairs. All the while I was being taught. There's a scripture that reads something like this, "once we are faithful in another's, then God will give us ours."

For me, it seemed to happen overnight. But I know that all those many years serving God was preparing me for His calling in a country that was last on my list to visit, working with kids. Though I liked kids, I was sure my calling in life was to work with men and men's issues. It was not to work with governments and churches, both of which I was not too keen on, or around a language that even after so many visits, I can't come close to speaking except a few words. Which one more time makes me rely, or may I use the word "submit," to others to help me.

When the decision was made that we needed to do something in Vietnam I began to call other organizations. Most just said, "Gosh that's wonderful, but you could just bring the funds to us." As I mentioned in another place, that wasn't what we wanted to do. We did find someone to work with and they began to mentor us as a part of their organization, maybe more than I had hoped. From the beginning I told them that we wanted to do our own organization. They helped us to find staff and we shared our office space with them. I watched and learned.

However, the things that I wanted to do, was to go beyond what they were doing. They were great at what they did, but the vision God had given me was to be more relational. I remember asking, "What happens to the kids living at this orphanage? How long can they live here?" I was told when they get to be 16 or 17 years old or graduate from high school, they leave and start their own life. The thought that hit me was that being a teenager is when they can really get into trouble, to make choices and not think of consequences that choice may have.

I could just imagine one of the girls leaving and somebody offering them a new pair of shoes and a new dress and oh yes, they have to go out with this man tonight. Or also many of the other things that can distract a teen. Of all the numbers that we have and they're quite extensive at this time, one of the ones I'm most proud of is how many graduates we have from universities and colleges. These are kids whose lives are transformed. And as exciting as that may be, even more so is that many come back after graduating our programs to talk and mentor kids who are going through what they did.

I saw how it was managed with the other organizations that I knew at the time. There was a "glass ceiling" so to speak. Even those that did have orphanages (which we called homes) only took care of kids for the short term. I do not want to take away from the many great organizations that do the relief and take care of children for the short term. There is a definite need for this. However, my wife's and my vision was to see lives that are transformed and this, in most cases, takes time.

I also learned that generally it is easier to raise funds for cute little kids than for someone older hoping to attend a university, college, or advanced level vocational school. None-the-less, we said let's do it!

How It Began?

My wife and I were unable to have children. I think guys don't have the inner drive to have children as much as women do. Sure, I wanted to have children and I thought it would be cool, but since we were unable to, that was OK also. We would be able to travel more, retire earlier or do other things together.

But for my wife it was different. She had a drive and a desire to have kids. We went to therapy. We learned that there's having our own children and then there's raising our own children.

We began investigating fertility treatments. We got to the point of in vitro and met with the doctors. They told us the cost was about $40,000 at that time and there's no guarantees. We had just enough money for either one in vitro treatment or an adoption. We decided to pray about it. A good friend of ours invited us to a charity event. The cost of the tickets was prohibitive for us at the time, but he invited us as his guests. We sat at his table and had a great evening. Our friend also bought us a ticket for the grand prize drawing, which was another thing I would never have risked the money on. That night we won the grand prize of two weeks in Costa Del Sol, Spain with round-trip airfare. Both Dorothea and I worked for our father's, so we decided to extend the trip by two more weeks and visit Italy and more of Spain.

On our return we stayed two nights in London. At the hotel I picked up the first English newspaper I had seen in a month. And there in the headlines was news that our doctor, whom we were supposed to do the in vitro with, had been arrested. When we met with him he told us that they had lots of frozen embryos that they cannot do anything with. They can do abortions regularly, but not dispose of embryos, only store them. He said what they decided to do was give them to other women who did not have any healthy eggs. Looking at the newspaper, I turned it around, showed it to my wife and said, "Here's our answer. I guess we'll be going down the adoption road."

Thinking back to what the therapist told us, we prayed about it and decided that we wanted to raise children. We hired one attorney, then a second attorney because it was taking too long. We met a couple of prospective birthmothers, but I questioned them about whether they really wanted to give up their child. I even spent time having lunch and talking with the bio-father. About three years went by and nothing happened.

We came home late one night after a friend's memorial service in the days of message machines. There was a message from one of our attorneys that said no matter what time we got home, to call him. We called and he then asked us to call another attorney. We learned about a young birth mother who decided to give up her 11 day old baby. The next day we met her and she agreed to let us adopt our son.

I remember the attorney looking at us and saying, "Do you have a carseat for the baby? You'll need it to bring him home." Puzzled, I looked at her and said, "You mean like today? Don't we need diapers and a place for him to sleep?" She replied, "Yes, is that going to be a problem?" I said, "No, there's a Costco on the way."

We met our son that afternoon. He was born two months premature weighing about 4 pounds and his lungs were not completely developed. The doctors wanted to keep him at the hospital for another day. My wife and I went out to dinner that night at a celebrated chef's restaurant. However, all I could do was just look at the food, one of the rare times I was unable to eat. The next day we picked up our son, Thomas. Because his lungs had not developed fully, he had to be connected to a monitor. The doctors at the hospital told us the monitor will tell you if he stops breathing. Me, the educated one, said to them, "What do you mean stop breathing?!"

He told us the monitor will start a loud beeping and you just have to tap him a little bit and he'll start breathing again. I have to say I was rather freaked out. What made it worse was they had set the alarm for a very low point, so that it literally would go off every half hour or 40 minutes all night long over the weekend. When I called the doctors on Monday they came and reset it, saying, "Sorry, it was set too low."

For the most part, our son Thomas spent the first few months sleeping on top of my chest. My son was a really good baby. He slept at night and as a toddler if you put him down in one place, he'd stay there. I was content, as I had a son. I was good, but my wife had this deep yearning. She wanted a second child and as you know, a happy wife is a happy life.

We once again began the adoption journey. Lawyers were looking and two and one half years had passed and nothing. My son was an exemplary child, yet my sweet wife Dorothea still yearned for a second child.

I came back from a men's event where I had been "thinking". I shared with my wife, I'm getting older and that it's not fair for a child to have such an old father. Truth be told I was thinking about myself. I was thinking when I could retire and when we could go on vacations. Really it was all about me and not so much about a potential second child. My wife looked at me and said, "OK, let me pray about it." The next morning what she said was in itself, a miracle. She said, "If it doesn't happen by my birthday, I will give up on another adoption." Her birthday was only two and one half months away. After all these years of pursuing fertility treatments and five and one half years on the adoption road, I figured we were done.

God had other plans. Five days later a phone number was put on her desk at work from someone who had adopted a child from Vietnam. She called the contact two days later and learned that he had not only adopted from Vietnam, but also served on a board of an organization that facilitated adoptions.

Next thing I knew we were getting off the plane in Saigon! I was hit by the heat, humidity, sites, sounds, and smells of Vietnam. It was not what I was used to growing up in Southern California. I remember looking at my wife and angrily saying, "What have you gotten me into?" Again, it was about me.

It was on that first day that we met our daughter at Go Vap Orphanage. It was a government run orphanage with about 270 children. I think at that time, about 60% of the children were disabled. My daughter, like many of the other children, had scabies and ringworm.

I clearly remember holding her up over my head that day and saying, "You have won the lottery. You are going to a country and a family where you'll have every opportunity in life." And being the dad that I am, I gave her her first lecture of, "what you do with it will be up to you."

We would visit her every day. The process at that time was you begin the paperwork and then 40 days later you receive your child at a giving and receiving ceremony. We were there for about two weeks. My wife and I ended up visiting other orphanages and handicap schools. I got to meet the other kids in the cribs next to her. I still get emotional even as I type this out at the memory. I am actually fighting back the tears.

We flew home and returned two weeks later. It was right before my daughter's first birthday. She turned one the day she was released to us. We had to remain in Vietnam for another 11 days.

During that time we ended up in even more handicap schools, orphanages and places with kids in desperate need of hope and opportunity. I remember looking at tourist guides and saying, "How come I'm not seeing the tourist points of interest, why am I ending up with all these kid things?" You see, I thought my calling was in the local church, in the local streets working with guys with guy stuff, like addictions, alcoholism, etc.

I mean I liked kids and all, but that was not my calling and I knew that. Then one day my wife met a lady in the gym at the hotel. She invited us to go out with her that day. Quite frankly, I was nervous being out on the streets. The chaos of all the traffic and the motorbikes was way beyond me. So, I was happy to go with someone that knew the area. She was a Vietnamese American that had been working in a prominent, well known computer software company.

Lo and behold, guess what? Yes, as promised she took us to a place she knew to get a good price on souvenirs, but we ended up at another orphanage. It was at a Buddhist temple orphanage with 112 girls outside of Saigon. I remember looking at the kids and comparing them to the orphanage my daughter was from. The one my daughter was from was a government run orphanage with no spirituality at all. The kids wore clothes that were relatively new, but they were dirty, tattered and some kids would only have one shoe. It was really the culture of the place. It seemed as though they just did the minimum to keep kids alive and old enough to move out of the orphanage, or for the luckier ones to be adopted.

At this Buddhist run orphanage, the kids' clothes were thin and worn, but they were all clean and neat. The oldest kids went to school and they had makeshift classes set up where they would teach the next younger ones. Each of the kids down to the youngest age had chores to do. There was discipline, which was quite the opposite of what I saw at my daughter's orphanage. I saw the benefit of an orphanage run with some spirituality, but it wasn't a spirituality that I was accustomed to or followed.

My wife Dorothea was chatting away as usual. She was one of the friendliest people around, loved all and was loved by all. I was standing by two rusty water tanks and I "told" God, "You need to get some Christians in here to do this," and I heard that whisper, "you're it!"

Honestly, I sorta freaked out. Call it what you will, but I had never heard a whisper that loud before.

Sure not really audible, but nonetheless, it was loud and in a tone I had not heard before.

I ran around the corner to where my wife was talking and I said, "Come on we're going!" She looked at me, noticing that I was a little freaked out. We got into a taxi and she asked, "What's wrong?" I said, "Never mind, never mind! I just want to get back to the hotel."

The giving and receiving ceremony happened and our daughter was now in our place, which was a makeshift apartment. Leaving the orphanage she didn't know how to crawl. I am guessing it was because she had been in a crib all her life. She did know how to stand up around the coffee table or any other furniture piece and walk around. Silly me, I taught her how to crawl. Her first word was "that!" She would point at something and say "that!" I would walk her over to it and she would touch it, laugh and then point at something else and say "that!" And we'd walk to it and she'd touch it, laugh and point at another thing and repeat.

Finally the time came for our flight home. I was soooo ready to be home and away from this country and back to the country I was "used" to. I remember packing and placing the suitcase right next to the door. I then sat down on the couch, turning the TV on. At that time the only English speaking channel was CNN news. I watched bewildered, not sure what I was seeing. At first, I thought it was some type of re-enactment of the old War of the Worlds radio show, where everybody panicked. What I was looking at was the twin towers, one with smoke billowing out of it. As I watched, I saw the second plane go into the building.

It was September 11, 2001 in the United States. I will forever remember where I was and how I felt. Even now there's tears.

As you know all flights to the US were canceled. My son was at home in the US and when I talked to him on the phone and he said, "Daddy is it true that there's some bad men that flew airplanes into buildings?" I answered, "Yes son" and he then asked, "and they haven't caught them yet?" I replied, "Yes son, that's true."

My heart was breaking and my old background was flaring up. I wanted to come home, get a gun and not only protect my home, but the homes of so many others in the United States. The journals I wrote at the beginning of our journey to adopt were just telling of our time in Vietnam, the traffic and the food. But from 9/11 on they turned to daily journals working to encourage the many people that were so distraught and in fear in the United States.

Five days later we were on the second flight out of Vietnam. For me, it was not a day too soon. Walking onto the plane I remember looking at my wife and boldly saying, "I'll never come back to this hell hole again!" I can just picture the laugh heaven got that day. I imagine Jesus gathering a few like Moses, Peter and others, giggling and pointing at me saying, "Watch this one! See what his destiny is." At the time of this writing I've been back to Vietnam, my second home, about 70 times. Yes, I did write my second home. So much for my best thinking!

What happened was when I returned to the US, I was literally haunted by the faces of the children I had met in the different orphanages and handicap schools. The question wouldn't leave my thoughts of what was their future? What is their destiny? I was actually haunted by the faces of the children I had seen, met and often played with. Yes, I held my daughter up and told her she had won the lottery going to a family and country where she would have every opportunity. But what about those kids that I have left behind? I believed that every child deserves a chance!

I was home for a couple weeks and then left for a Men's Conference. Robert Barriger from Peru, spoke at one of the sessions. I had met him in the past and wanted to go up and thank him and say hi. As I walked up, I noticed him talking to two of the large supporters of that ministry and thought I'm not going to disturb them right now. But just as I walked past them I heard Barriger say, "...that's the problem with orphanages."

Though I was several steps past them, I turned around then asked Barriger, "What's the problem with orphanages?" He said "staffing," then looking at me, he stepped between the two other men, rather close to me. Then asked, "Robert do you know the difference between a burden and a calling?" Although I wanted to sound spiritual, like I knew the answer, I got honest and said, "no I don't."

He said, "A burden is when someone goes to another country or to another place and does some good work. But the heat, the humidity, the sites, the smells, the sounds, the stomach sickness, all get to them. When he returns home the first place he goes to eat is a fast food restaurant. He hears of someone else going to the same place and he says, here's some money and I'll pray for you." At this point he had me nodding, that was my story!

Then he began to describe a calling. "That's where God sends someone someplace. The heat, the humidity, the sights, the sounds, the stomach illness all hit this person also. But when he returns home, all he can do is remember the faces." Even as I write this, a flood of emotion hits me and I'm fighting off tears. I still remember the faces of the kids I met on that first trip in 2001. Visiting the orphanages I remember the feelings and emotions I was haunted with when I returned.

As Barriger spoke to me, tears welled up from my deepest emotions. It had been two weeks since I returned home and I couldn't stop thinking about those kids, the kids we left behind— what was their future? Surely they didn't have the opportunities my daughter would have and every child deserves a chance!

When I came home from the conference, right away I went to my wife, Dorothea. I looked her in the eyes and said, "Honey, I think we're supposed to do something in Vietnam." Now I know, because of the sweetness of my wife, that she didn't use these words, but basically she looked me in the face and said "DUH!"

So we began and honestly I had absolutely no idea about non-profits or what or how to begin. All I knew is if this was God or a "calling," I didn't want to miss the opportunity. For years I've been serving in other ministries, helping other people. I'd hear people talking about dreams and visions and I wondered, where is mine? Sure, God used me. I was of service in many areas, but somehow in my heart, in my gut, I felt that there was more that God had for me to do.

I began by talking to others, and quite frankly there wasn't a lot of encouragement. In fact it was mostly discouragement. Some would say, "Why do it there? If you do it in the US I'd fund it." I just knew that I had heard God's voice, or at least thought I heard His calling. I'd rather be called a fool one more time, than miss something that God had asked me to do.

Okay now what? I called other organizations and talked to them. Several told me, "Well that's wonderful, but you don't have to reinvent the wheel. Just bring your funds to us and you can do the work."

During our adoption process we came across a need of the handicap school for some equipment for physical therapy. A good friend of mine said, "I'll pay for it." So I gave the funds to the organization that was handling our adoption. After all, they had introduced us to the need. I explained to them very clearly that I would need a paper trail. I needed receipts, I needed photos, I needed documentation.

Several months had gone by and I had not received anything. And as I have mentioned in other places, I sorta grew up on the streets and had trust issues. Compound that with my father telling me growing up, "Don't trust anybody."

So I knew that my wife and I had to start our own organization. I kept calling around and I found one guy out of North Carolina and in his southern accent he said, "that's wonderful! Make sure you do this, then have this done and get this done and when you get to this office in Vietnam, mention my name as he's a good friend."

I told my wife I think we found a partner, but let's fly out and meet him. I need to find out where his heart and motives are. We got there and went into his living room and he stood up and said, "Do you mind if we begin with prayer?" He was a fine southern gentleman. So we began Giving it Back to Kids.

I knew I had to set up a board, so I went to the busiest people I knew and asked them to serve. I'd go up to them and say, "I want to talk to you about your spare time." They looked at me like I was nuts. Maybe I was, a little anyways for sure. I told them that I want to transform kids' lives, and to give kids in Vietnam a chance! I'd share about what my idea and vision was and they smiled at me and said, "OK I'm in."

As I thought more about it, I began to wonder how are we going to fund this thing? As I pondered the problem, I knew five people of means who came to mind. I thought, well they could fund it for the first year. The funny thing is, none of them give any funds the first year.

I felt with the people I knew from my different contacts that we could make a good run for 2 to 3 years. The truth is Giving It Back To Kids didn't begin to grow until after the third year. Call it what you will, but I think from the beginning it was God showing me this is His thing and He will grow it.

It was in the third year that Giving It Back To Kids began to show noticeable growth. Those that I had thought would help fund the organization the first year, all came back in following years asking me, "Why don't you ask us for money?" Truth is I did and they told me no!

The rest is history and maybe material for another book. There were lots of learning opportunities, some of which were so painful that I want to slap myself in the back of the head. In the following pages I've tried to write down some lessons I've learned or am learning, which is probably more accurate.

Also, there are a few of the lessons I hope I have learned from my failures. I by no means want to come across as an expert in any way. If you could see inside my head, you know that's the last thing I feel. As I said in other parts of this book, if I can do it, surely you can too! My hope by writing these lessons is it might help in some small way to get you to a spot, or maybe you won't have to pay as much duty to cross the borders into success.

To be honest, as I've reread this I realize it might be better said and kept at "lessons I am learning." What's key is that I remember to keep learning. I wish I could say that once I learned these lessons I was done, but that's not the case. I find myself learning some of them over and over, but at least it's less often. As I've said before, it's progress rather than perfection. One of the great things is this, when I do make a mistake and it affects somebody else, I have the wonderful tool of going back and saying, "Hey I'm sorry, I was wrong, please forgive me," and have even added, "what can I do to make it right?"

I began to wonder, how do I do charity work? What do I do and how?" You see running a non-profit was never in the scope of my imagination of something I would ever do. It definitely was not leading a humanitarian organization, much less in Vietnam! As I wondered and prayed I heard a God whisper, if I can be so bold to say. It was to do for the kids in our programs the same as I'd do for my own kids.

Kids need different things at different times. Sometimes they need to go to the doctor. Get them healthy, have surgery, immunizations or any of the other needs for sick kiddos. Other times they need a bike to get to school or a college education. They need to learn about discipline and training to be a responsible adult.

So we began. I am not aware of any other organizations working in Vietnam that puts braces on kids. Sure it doesn't save a life, but gosh it's life-changing. It changes them from lowering their heads and not being willing to smile and frowning, to adopting a huge smile and looking people straight in the eyes. It provides confidence in themselves.

One thing I had never realized came from the first girl we put braces on. I remember looking at her one time and thinking she sure could use braces. I didn't say anything, thinking that's a crazy idea. The next day I saw her and she asked to practice speaking English with me. As we worked on pronunciation she lowered her head shaking it and saying, "Darn, because of my teeth I can't pronounce this letter." It was then I realized we had to put braces on her and she now has a beautiful smile, is confident and works as an interpreter in many situations, including being a guide. From the beginning I remember people looking at me and saying, "Wouldn't you be better served if you picked one thing and did that well?" For us, I'm not sure for you, I said; "We did! We picked one thing, kids!"

If my vision is something I can figure out how to get to, it's probably an insult or makes God laugh, because it's certainly not big enough for him. Too often I have heard people say, "Here's my plan or vision and this is how we're going to accomplish it." Sounds good at first thought, but then I begin to ask if it's big enough or wide enough? Is it something that only if God steps in, will it get accomplished?

For us to begin what we did was huge, an undertaking that most scoffed at. Many worked to persuade us to look to partner with local organizations or churches, letting them do the heavy lifting and us supporting. And this may just be a perfect place for you. We actually did just that for the first handful of years. For us, we knew we had to be on our own and totally trust God to accomplish our goals by bringing others in who'd share the same dreams.

I recognize and readily admit that not everyone is called to go do something like Giving It Back To Kids in Vietnam. But I really feel that each of us, everyone of us, has something we can do to make a difference in other people's lives. What's yours?

Lessons Learned

Things I know, things I don't know and thirdly what I don't know that I don't know. This book is just a beginning for me in learning. I hope to share something that might inspire others to make a difference, to live a life of significance. I wish I could say that I have these lessons down, but surely that is not the case. It seems in the writing of this book I have been tested in all of them. Some I did ok others... well, not so much.

It Is Not About Me or GIBTK.

It does not matter, nor should it ever matter, that GIBTK or I get credit for something someone else does from our idea. It is about fulfilling vision and dreams, about building kingdoms. It is building and spreading the culture God entrusted us with.

If I really believe our culture and methods are good, then I need to be ecstatic that it spreads, that others take it on, call it their own and don't give us the credit. It may very well be my ego that I or GIBTK need to be recognized. Honestly it has been and I hate to admit it, hard at times to see someone we trained, supported or invested our time, talents and treasure into, take the "culture" of GIBTK and begin their own organization or go to another organization. But truth be told, the need for change and the spread of what God gave is too big. It must be carried on way beyond the borders of our organization.

Training Others

I'm reminded of the time I visited an orphanage just outside of the Danang area. A few years before we'd visit and support an orphanage a couple hours outside of our office city of Danang. The kids were unruly. The staff that worked there, well I couldn't say they were hard-working. There would always be dust and dirt everywhere and not just a little bit, but layers of it. I remember on several consecutive visits over the course of a year, in one of the bathrooms there was a giant spider web with a spider about an inch and half. It had made a home there and nobody bothered to clean it. I would go to give an unconditional father's hug to the kids and they would run away. I'd have to chase them down or give up.

We did finally stop supporting this orphanage because we found out that most of the vitamins we donated were going out the back door and being resold. Some time had passed and somehow I heard that a number of those children, those over eight years old, had been moved to an orphanage outside of Danang. I said, "Let's visit there." As the van pulled into the courtyard one of the kids from the prior orphanage saw me and let out this, for lack of a better way to say it, almost an animal scream. Next thing I knew I saw 14 kids running to the van. As I type this I'm brought to tears again.

While I'm getting out of the van the kids were coming up to me, those same kids that used to run from me and hide to get away from that father's hug. "We're coming up and getting our hugs!" they said, pointing to themselves and saying the name of the city and orphanage where I had met them before. They wanted to be recognized. We spent a couple hours there. At one point I remember looking and recognizing the fact that even though I thought we were not making a difference at that other place, we were.

I remember looking out, having several kids around me hugging me and sitting on my knee and saying, "there's no way, there's too many kids and I only have so many arms."

It was at that point I realized, and I need to remind myself, that it's only by training others to train others to learn the culture of the organization and carrying it on, that the dream I have been entrusted with of transforming a region, can ever happen.

Don't Be Focused On Money

When I first began in the non-profit arena, I found myself way too eager to meet people of financial means with available money. I'd see someone walk in and key in that I needed to find the moment to share about GIBTK and "let them know" how they can "partner" with us. I felt as though I would shake their hand with one hand and with the second hand be reaching into their pockets. I felt dirty, dishonest. I would often be reminded at times like these, of verses where it talks about a wealthy person walking in and bringing them to the front, treating them special. I realized I had to make changes. The scripture reading of the woman that brought a mite for her offering is still talked about. What she gave represented more of a gift of her life's worth than the many much larger gifts.

I remember in the early days we had the opportunity to set up a table for a mission fair at my local church. I had video, photos, brochures and of course donation envelopes ready. Some came and talked, others gave, but one older lady broke me. Even as I write I'm fighting back tears.

From the sight of her she very well might have been homeless. She wore a "not so clean" pink coat. She told me how much she loved what we did and wanted to help. I thanked her and asked that she pray for us, that it is the prayers that keep us going. She smiled and said I want to do more. (Honestly I wanted to give her some money). Out of one pocket she pulled a $1 bill and from her "not so clean" left sleeve she pulled another $1! Honestly it has been over 15 years since it happened, yet I'm flooded with emotions. My thoughts that day as well as today, was that I had met a modern day widow giving her mite.

The lesson is that I need/must learn and practice that every gift is truly appreciated and not to value one gift over another. Not to give more time to someone who may be able to "help" more. I laugh thinking about this. I can't help wonder if maybe, just maybe, God sends those to us to see how we will react. What is it that our actions say? Do we really care for the person or for their money and what they can bring us? Do we really trust God to provide? For us and GIBTK, it has been all Him!

Don't pick boards and advisory members for what they can bring financially. I know this goes contrary to wise advice. However, I have been called and called myself, a "contrarian" on more than one occasion. It is easy to bring someone on who is successful in hopes that they will bring donors. It really does make sense. I do see that many of those I serve with on the GIBTK board are successful in business. So I say this with caution.

I am reminded of a trip I lovingly call "the trip from hell." I had set up an 'advisory' board. Made up of men who were successful and known for their giving in hopes of increasing the donations received by GIBTK. I asked for the advisory board as well as a couple board members to join this trip. My hope was for them to come and see what GIBTK was doing and how. These guys came with 'fire hoses' to put out fires. Unfortunately for them and fortunately for GIBTK, there were no fires really. What I had hoped for was for the trip to be a come, see and learn; then return home, think and then further discuss. There was nothing to fix, which is what they came to do.

My back went out. The "guys" had sidebar meetings without me, discussing what they perceived as the problems of GIBTK. At one point I was confronted by several who questioned me about how we could fund a compassion house for a poor family when GIBTK was in crisis! Funny thing is I had not received that memo! GIBTK was fine and there was no crisis I was aware of. On that trip one board member came up behind me and quietly whispered in my ear. "Don't forget this is your baby, you're the leader!" Before the end of the trip I had written my resignation letter.

Upon our return I realized my mistakes. The first was never to pick a board for funding, but rather for character and what they bring organizationally. Secondly, this is one learning opportunity I believe God took me to the woodshed over. I felt as though God was saying, "If you're going to lead, then lead! If not get out of the way." I saw that I "thought" we were a bunch of good ol' boys getting together to help kids in Vietnam. Just a bunch of guys doing good. But what GIBTK required was a leader.

Once we returned I had personal meetings with each of the guys on that trip. I apologized to them (because I was in error) for not being a leader. That I had mistakenly given the impression that I had not understood where GIBTK was. I told them I wanted to be clear in that I knew where GIBTK came from, where it is today and where we are headed. I also understood why they would step down. My lesson is bring on board members based on character, for their gifting and strength, not for funding.

Difference Between Managers and Leaders
Every organization needs both, a visionary that leads
and managers that manage.

One day over lunch a friend asked me if I had
ever heard of "The Masters Program," led by Bob
Shank. I looked a bit puzzled since just that morning
someone had emailed me about it. I said, "Yes, I have."
He said I believe you need to do this so much so that I
will pay your tuition for the first year. I signed up for
the 4 year Leadership Program.

On the first day, the leader Bob Shank, looked
us over and said, "If you're here, either you think or
someone you know, thinks you're a leader. If you are a
leader and are doing something someone else can do,
STOP IT!"

At the time I was typing out every thank you
letter for donations and all the clerical and admin
work. Please note, I type with the two finger method,
with many back spaces and deletes. It was a very slow
and time consuming chore for me. Within a couple
days after Bob shared about stopping doing things
others can do, I was sitting in front of my computer
typing thank you letters when I received a call. It was
from a local pastor. He shared that after his last
Sunday's sermon two young people came to him with
tears in their eyes. They told him they wanted to go
internationally and make a difference, that they felt
called. The pastor told me someone he knew said I
might be able to help. The pastor asked to meet with
me. I looked at the pile of thank you letters (it was
right after our annual fundraiser) that I still had to type

out. I told him the soonest I could meet was about 10 days from then. He thanked me and said he would call back if he did not find something sooner.

He never called back. I'm not sure if those young people got what they needed or not. One thing for sure is it made me realize that there are people who type much better than me and do a better job. I stepped out and found an assistant that could help, which freed me up to do things I was better at. Maybe even do things that only I could do for our organization.

This has continued to this day. I share this with all our team members as well. The problem with this is I have to give up control. The plus in this is others get to step up and make a difference as well. I had to get rid of the old adage of, it's easier if I do it myself! Yes it may take longer to train others, yes for sure there may be mistakes. But for honest growth of myself and others, giving up control and actually delegating rather than just using the term, makes for a healthier organization.

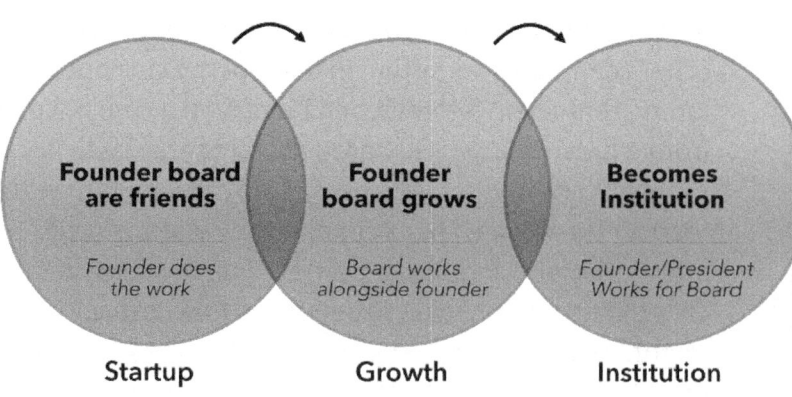

Founder board are friends	Founder board grows	Becomes Institution
Founder does the work	Board works alongside founder	Founder/President Works for Board
Startup	Growth	Institution

The first circle is the Startup Phase. Often the board is picked from friends. In this phase the founder does the work. The second circle is where the board works alongside the founder. The last circle is where the organization becomes an Institution. In this phase the founder works for the board. In each of the circles there is a bit of overlap.

When the organization goes from each level there is a time where the board still follows the founder but begins to have more input. Then the organization moves from board- founder led, to a board where the founder still has input and influence into decisions.

This may be a good time to say at this point GIBTK may need to look more like an equally run organization with the Board and founder working together, perhaps a time to bring on a board whose gifts fit into the future of GIBTK; things like promotion and professional development, aka a fundraiser.

Keeping The Vision and Culture

As Giving It Back To Kids has gotten larger and larger, the challenge is to keep the vision and culture. I just spoke about the concentric circles and recognized that in order for this organization to go way beyond my time on this earth, it had to be set up to be run by a board. To be honest, just the sound of that makes me cringe inside. Dare I say I need to give up control... but I recognize that I have to let go of this baby that I nurtured for so many years. Truth be told, this is where I am at in the writing of this book. Looking to expand the board and set up committees, including development. I am reminding myself to look for character, gifting and talents and not to look for the deep pockets potential board members might know.

I had to decide what the goal was for the organization. This was a question I was asked when we first were organizing Giving It Back To Kids. What was I looking for, short term or thinking I expected to see the vision of Giving It Back To Kids going on past my years? Well honestly when I think about it going beyond my years, especially in those early days, I just kind of wanna lower my head and say, "Gosh, how could that ever happen?" But as the years have passed, I see that it is a reality for the organization. And especially, the effects Giving It Back to Kids programs have had on the kids and yes, even the culture of S.E. Asia. As I pondered it, I realized I'm looking for long-term as an organization and in each of the kids and families we work with and that's where we came to the fact that we had to build an infrastructure.

Building Infrastructure

As I began to think about starting an organization to transform kids lives I sought out wise counsel. A friend, one of the best minds I know, met with me often. On one occasion he shared with me how in a physics class his University professor talked about a movie called 'Attack of the Giant Ants'. His professor told them that it was impossible for the ants to be the size they were in the movie. Okay, I was wondering what in the world this had to do with setting up a humanitarian organization. His professor went on to say that the body size of the ant could not physically be held up by the size of the ants legs. I left that meeting wondering what in the world was he talking about. And as so often happens, I realized the meaning several days later. He was telling me that the infrastructure of the organization has to be larger, or better put, stronger than needed, to carry the size of the organization. That before we grow we need to always be sure that the infrastructure or "legs" are in place or the body of the organization will collapse.

Importance of infrastructure and training became very clear in another way when my wife passed away after her battle with cancer in 2015. I was broken, as well as my son and daughter. I had to heal and more importantly, I had to be there for my children. It was then that I saw the importance of the infrastructure that we had spent so much time building. The staff stepped in and for the most part took care of the day-to-day stuff without any or very little input from me. GIBTK didn't lose a step.

Outgrow Me

In one of my meetings with my wise friend in the earliest days of GIBTK, he looked across the table at me and said, "You do know that one day GIBTK will outgrow you?" I was taken aback, wondering what he meant. Bravely I asked and he replied, "That with my education and experience that GIBTK, if it does grow, will need to have someone of more experience and education then I." Well honestly this was 2002, and that still has a sting to me. I remember thinking what do you mean? Take my baby from me! But my take away was that I had to become a learner. I must increase my knowledge of leadership, and the nonprofit world. To learn about working in a cross-culture world. Be a learner.

It's written in the Bible, God is made strong in our weakness. He just looks for the willing. But willingness without action is nothing but a fantasy. I had to be willing, but I also had to train myself to become a learner, to be a reader. To seek out podcasts, teaching and training. To set time to put myself into situations to learn. Learn to ask key questions from those who are more learned and experienced than me. To make learning a part of my life and not give up or quit. To not ever think, "I got this!" Continue being a learner.

Jack Welch's famous quote: "If change is happening outside the organization faster than it is on the inside, the end is near."

I think this quote not only speaks to our organizations, but also to each of us individually. I and GIBTK need to stay green and grow. Learning should never end. Learning can be a lot like riding a bicycle, as long as you keep pedaling you're fine, when you stop pedaling that is when you can fall off. I need to stay and be a learner and if I'm not learning anything I'm not growing. Yes there's going to be mistakes as I learn new things, but I remind myself to stay green, and try them anyway. As I often say, "If I or those on our team don't make mistakes, they are not trying anything new."

Dr. Cole always said, "The only constant in life is change, no matter how much we learn or how good we are at what we do." The times, cultures and needs all change. If we are not learning new things we become stale or stagnant and fall behind or out of place. We no longer fill the needs of the day.

No matter how many things I've learned or think I learned, I find out I still have more to learn. It is often like the layers of an onion. With each layer of the onion, I get deeper, we get deeper. You look at the onion and say, ok I see it. There it is, but until you begin to peel the layers, will you see that it keeps going deeper and deeper.

So it has been with my life. I remind myself every day that I need to learn and that I need to grow. I need to die to myself, and more often than not, die to old ideas and ways of working. Maybe better said, grow and mature in our old ideas and ways of work, that I or GIBTK has not arrived. Sure I've learned a lot, but I have so much more to learn. During the writing of this book I scoff at myself, questioning what do you think you're doing? Who are you to write a book? But it's not me, it's Him who is in me. I'm getting down some of the lessons that I've been made aware of. Rather than saying "lessons I've learned", is "lessons

I'm learning." Saying I've learned can mean I've got it, when in each of these things so often I fall short, because when another layer of the onion is peeled back, there's another level that I'm trying to work out.

The World and Culture Change

I was just recently made aware of the rate that knowledge is growing at. In the year 2019 knowledge doubled in the world. It is forecast in the not too distant future that knowledge will double every 12 hours. The influence of the internet is key to this. The need to learn and and stay ahead of those we lead is ever more important. If not I recognize those following will outgrow and turn to other ways and places to use their knowledge. They will get bored. They will not be challenged.

One of my friends is a high level official in Vietnam. He has met with US presidents and countless leaders from the US and other world leaders. He is also a wordsmith. When we talk, it's easy to see that he thinks about and measures every word he plans to use before he actually uses it. His English speaking and vocabulary is exceptional, yet when speaking it was easy to see each word was thought of before escaping his lips. One day I was asking him if he could help us. I was looking to expand our distribution of wheelchairs into Cambodia.

I asked if maybe the Vietnam government would like to be part of the process helping to "bridge" the two countries. He corrected me, saying not to use the word bridge. He said the word bridge implies a gap between something. That one simple lesson I wish I could say changed me.

Too often I get to talking with all my energy and passion about GIBTK and so many other topics, that words I use may convey a different meaning then I intend. Yes, since that conversation I do "try" to think before the words spill out of my mouth. As another friend says, "pump the brakes" before speaking. In another part of this book it suggests to pause before speaking, especially when agitated or feeling a need to defend something I've done or said.

Communication Is The Basis Of Life

We need to continue, I need to continue to become a better communicator. One of the tools in communication is to engage those I'm communicating with, or at least trying to communicate with, by asking questions. I'm learning to and most often remind myself to ask questions. Rather than teach or preach what I want said, I've found myself often answering or teaching what I think people need to know, when that's really not where they're at. Perhaps they need to hear something more basic on the team or they already understand this and have some other questions.

Some of the best communicators I know, when I sit down with them, one on one, they ask questions. They get me to think, and often I come up with the answer. Or what's more likely, is they lead me to the answer and let me think I came up with it. Remembering to ask questions makes those, or helps those I was trying to communicate with, to feel they are a part of, to own it. To know that they matter, that what they think and want to know is important to me also. That what I'm trying to communicate is not this is what Robert says, but more of let's talk about this, let's come up with answers. To come up with solutions, let's agree on what needs to be talked about.

Dr. Cole taught a long time ago, agreement is the place of power. If I'm communicating one thing and the team is hearing another, or whoever I'm talking to is closed off, is not listening or thinking he just doesn't get it, I'm not getting anywhere.

We communicate with words, gestures and spirit. The lowest form of communication is assumption. In today's day of emails and texts, so much can and does get lost, and worse misinterpreted. Our communication becomes unclear and lost all too often because of the lack of gesture and spirit. To better communicate it requires all three.

In our busy world it is all too simple to fire off a text or email, rather than take or make the time for face to face conversation. Even in today's world, actual phone calls are becoming less and less common. I am totally guilty of this. It is an area I myself am aware of and need to work at being better at. We also have things like FaceTime that can help clear up confusion and misunderstanding in our communication.

There's Listening

Communication is also a two-way street. Listening... I hesitate to even speak on this matter, much less put it in writing. It is something I still struggle with. I've begun to understand for many such as myself, listening does not come naturally. It is an acquired skill. For me it takes conscious effort. Too often when someone is speaking I'm waiting for them to finish (or take a breath) so I can have my turn to speak. I am thinking about what I want to say. Or while listening, thinking I already know what they're saying and already have their answer or my rebuttal, without really listening to them all the way through. Or often, frankly I don't care what they're saying cause I'm thinking about what I "need" to do next, or about the store I have to stop at on the way home.

What I have found useful is to stop whatever I'm doing, focus on the person speaking, looking them in the eyes. If sitting I practice placing my hands in front of me, often fingertips and palms together. This posture helps my brain slow down and just listen.

Often I've found people aren't looking for answers they just need or want someone to listen, to care about them. It validates them. I've also learned to say things like I can see how you feel that way. Or if it is directed at me, or confrontational, "Gosh, let me think about that," or "You may be right, let me think about that." Most importantly is to learn and practice being a listener. I know I sure do love and need to be heard. After reading this last section I see how often I use the word "I", and looking back realize that perhaps listening is really an "I" problem. Additionally, perhaps my focus is on myself rather than the person I'm listening to.

Pause

Now this is an interesting word for me, since I am a shoot from the hip type guy. You know— the ready, shoot, aim type. Pause, it's not something I often do or did. But I'm learning unfortunately, through making mistakes. When I have opportunities to consider, rather than just going for the first thought that I have, (too often charged with emotion I may feel or "old" thinking), I "try" to make myself stop for a few days or at least a day and think about it. Often I try talking to others, find wise counsel with someone that I've been in a relationship with that either knows me or understands the situation.

I can't tell you how many times I've sent an email or a text message and wish I could pull it back. Rereading the words, we see that the intent or spirit of what we're attempting to say was not transmitted. When we pause it's not that we're putting off what can happen. Very often it's more that we are waiting for more information, or for additional direction from God.

Putting The Cart Before The Horse

I am so guilty of that. Way too often as visionaries we see where we're headed. We know the destination. God gives us a vision and that's when we should pause and wait for Him, for the correct timing. I often pray and look for closed doors rather than open doors. There seems to be never ending open doors. We've been invited to so many different parts of the world, from Africa to South America to India. For a number of years I received regular emails stating the Orphan's of Mumbai are waiting for you, please come. I hope honestly I didn't miss the open door God had for us, but I'm fairly sure if we were supposed to be there we would've been there. Our calling as far as this one can see, is Southeast Asia.

I need to always try to find the right time before I charge, before I get my team to charge. And then there's times where the doors open and the timing is right. We go through the door, yet once we go through it, it's very slow going. For my type of personality that is very difficult. I expect once it's time, everything is supposed to fall in place in front of us and make a clear path. But the truth is that we have often found that we have to clear the path. We have to build relationships and truly seek out where we are best to serve.

I am the kind of person that when I see something that needs to be done, I charge in and get it done or at least try to get it done. The truth is as visionary's or leaders we often will see where we're headed or destinations. I need to pause and wait for timing, for guidance, for wisdom. Not to get the cart before the horse.

Much like the GPS in my car, I can key in an address because I know where I'm going. However, I need the GPS to help guide me there. So it is in leadership— I need people and navigators that'll direct and help us get to our destination. And much like driving, you can rush to get to your destination and hit rush-hour traffic, or when possible, you can adjust your timing for a smoother, easier and more timely ride.

As leaders we see the next destination, the next program, the next thing that we want to do and we encourage and drag our team to the summit. Once they come to the top of that hill, after going through the valleys, tired, scraped up and bruised, what's the "natural" thing a leader does? He points to the next summit, the next destination, the next program. A leader has been thinking about it for some time. They are the visionary.

One of my big challenges is to pause, to relax a little bit to think of the team and in what it takes for them to get to these summits. Way too often the team will follow me as a leader because they trust me and quite frankly I am the boss. Unfortunately they don't see the vision and they don't see the new program. We need reminders to always be thoughtful and mindful of the team, giving breaks, days off and always encouraging.

As leaders we are to show the way, to shed light on the path that often very few or no one has traveled. Then to take that path to new levels, programs, needs, etc. Sometimes I can see myself being, for lack of a better word, a light. We're able to shed light on "new ground."

Stop and think for a second, when in a dark room even a little bit of light can help us to see and to move forward, hopefully avoiding obstacles. Then again, have you ever been in a room where the light is malfunctioning, having a buzz to it or making a noise and how annoying it gets? Or how about while driving at night, especially on a dark road, and an oncoming car's high beam lights blind you for a moment? So it can be with those we lead, not to be so bright that we blind those we are leading, or making so much noise that we have become annoying. A leader makes the path clear for others to follow, and even allows for them to make mistakes.

Doing the type of work we do as leaders, or as parents, it's easy to forget about ourselves. Think about the safety announcement they give before a plane takes off. One of the first things they say is, "if an emergency happens, an oxygen mask will drop from the ceiling." They then say we must put the oxygen mask on ourselves first before we help anybody else, even our own children.

Quite honestly, if my child was sitting next to me I think I would be tempted to put a mask on them first. How often is that the case in our lives? We're running around so busy helping others doing the good work that we forget about ourselves. We need to take the things that fill us up and fill our tanks up. Much like an airplane when it runs out of fuel, it's gonna come to a crash landing and so it is with us.

I heard a speaker talk on this. He asked us to make a list of the things that drain our "tanks". That was easy! Next he asked us to make a list of the things that fill our "tanks." Honestly, I have a hard time even to this day to know the things that fill me. It's so easy doing the good work that we do, to get so busy that we forget to put the oxygen mask on ourselves first. It's vitally important to take care of ourselves, making sure "our own tanks" are full.

You can't give something you don't have; whether it be about culture, emotional health or life skills, the list goes on. If it is just taught and not genuinely owned, too often the teaching just falls to the ground. Oh they might pass a test on the material, but the heart does not change. I've heard it said the 18 inches between your brain and your heart can be the longest distance. Whenever we've brought in new ideas such as emotional health, we begin with the team leaders, working with them to train them and then move onto the team itself. Next comes the house moms, then finally the kids in our homes. Using this method it becomes more genuine.

Let's go back to the saying, "I can't hear what you're saying because your actions are too loud." If you have somebody talking about healthy conversation, or difficult conversation, or how to control your anger and you see them angry and not having that difficult conversation, it's hard to believe it's real. This is not easy, especially with some of our leadership team and kids that have been through serious trauma. Trauma, which honestly I couldn't even begin to understand what it must be or feel like.

It's easy to gloss over hurt in our lives and not own it. What has happened is that we are far from perfect. There are many situations I look at from afar and see they still have some more processing to do. Local government has heard about our emotional health and our life skills programs and shown interest in them. So much so that as of this writing we are currently teaching emotional health and soft skills in 30 elementary and mid-level schools and three universities. Trust me, there's that word trust again and in order for kids to believe, much less make the necessary changes or take the right action, they have to believe the person speaking is genuine.

Nothing works better than someone speaking from experience. When someone says, "Oh, that must be terrible, or I know how you feel," but has never experienced it, it can almost feel like an insult. It can be more hurtful than good. However when you can look someone in the eye and say, "I know how you feel, I've been there, here's my story," it makes all the difference. To be genuine, honest and open sure adds validity and usefulness if one has processed their own stuff first.

Encouragement
This is something that I have to be very clear about. I need to remind myself to constantly encourage team members. They get tired and worn out. Way too often if one does not recognize and acknowledge team members they feel unappreciated. They burn out and can leave. A simple line of encouragement can keep their tanks full. It can be something as simple as just walking into the office and going to their desk and saying a few simple words.

Another aspect we've been trying to incorporate into our culture is for team members to encourage each other. We even strive and often need to remind each other to write a simple note of encouragement to a team member. Maybe it is something one did to help another this week. Doing this helps to keep our tanks full.

Running With The Wind or Against The Wind

My friend Bob Shank used this analogy the first time I heard it. Bob is a marathon runner. He says when training, "I always look to see which way the wind is blowing and my preference is always running with the wind to my back. When it is at my back it just pushes me along in the direction I'm going. Sometimes the wind can hit me to the side, but I keep running my route. What does happen is sometimes I'm pushed by the wind to the left or to the right. I can become a little off course, but remind myself to correct if needed. The days when I encounter a head wind, a wind coming straight at me, most often I will change course. If I have to go in the direction that I was going I'll take an angle at it rather than going into it head on."

He went on to say that's the same thing in leadership. We need to be aware which way the wind is coming. Are we fighting a headwind and should we adjust the course just a little bit to hit it at an angle? A side wind in our leadership can buffet us, but we stay on course. And of course there have been times in leading GIBTK that we have the wind to our backs and gosh, that's the fun times.

I heard that a friend of mine from Peru, who has a large church presence in South America, asked another friend, "Why does it have to be so hard?" His friend answered, "Because you're trying to transform a nation!" Often I've asked myself the same thing. The answer I came up with was, if it's not hard anybody could do it. It's the challenges of leadership. In the early days when I used to call this friend in South America, one time I asked him, "Does it ever feel like you're in over your head?" His answer..."once you're over your head it doesn't matter how deep the water is!" At which point I looked at the phone and thought, this was worth a long distance call? Yes it was worth the call. Just knowing that someone with a very successful organization and ministry sometimes felt like it was over his head and that at times felt it was too hard, gave me enough to keep going.

Another time I called him and asked, "Do you ever feel like quitting?" His response, "How many times a day do you think about quitting?" Again knowing that this well respected leader has times which they find challenging, encouraged me.   Dr. Cole put it this way, "Champions are not those who don't fail, they are those who don't quit." The same could be said about leaders. Successful or dare I say great leaders, all have problems, all encounter headwinds, side winds and challenges that may make them want to just bury their face in their hands or head in the sand. However they get up and they keep proceeding forward, maybe taking a different angle on the course. They bring others around them that they are in a relationship with, that will help them make it up the steepest of hills or mountains and overcome many obstacles.

Too often we are against what we do not understand. And or when something new comes up, a new way to do things, a new program or way to do it, my first reaction is "No! That's not for us." Or, "that's not how we've always done it. Let's remember what got us here, so we MUST keep doing it the same." These days the reaction I strive for is, "let me think about it." Pause, get counsel, which means listen to others' thoughts and input. This is especially true of those who know me, know GIBTK and those I am in relationship with.

This is also the case when one of my children or kids in one of our homes, does something that I'm unhappy with and I want to react. One of my mentors told me, "Robert, you need to disarm your reactors. Turn them into responders." Honestly with me, pausing has "almost" become a habit. I always thought being impulsive and ready to go at the drop of a hat was cute, likable or the way to be.

One thing I need to be careful of though, is that I don't use pause as a way of putting off something I'm not sure I want to do or being lazy about. I need to strive to always take action or the next indicated step.

One thing I just mentioned is talk to wise counsel. The key part of this is that you have to have wise counsel with those that you have built relationships with, people that know you and have a fair idea of who you really are or of the work you do.

This does not come easily for me. I tend to have a low fence to get to meet me, but a very high fence to protect getting to know me. I do have some that are close to me on a personal type level, and those on the professional level. There are a couple in the professional level that know me personally as well. It is this way that when things come up, others' ideas etc., I can "pause" and talk to my circle of friends, thereby making a clear and hopefully better decision.

Wake Up Other's Dreams

One of my passions has been to stir up and wake up dreams in others. Even in the writing of this book my hope is that others who have a "dream," but are hesitant to take steps to achieve it, might take the next indicated step. Not to "pause," waiting for a "better" time. Often people get stumped and are scared to take steps towards their dreams. There is fear of failure and often fear of success. They feel ill equipped, not ready, too young, too old, married or not yet married, kids are too young, the list can go on and on.

I often talk to people about a story in the New Testament. There's a storm at sea. The disciples are in the boat alone and Jesus walks to them on water. At first the disciples are scared. Peter speaks up first saying, "Lord if it's you, tell me to come." Jesus said "come" and Peter got out of the boat taking a few steps and sank. Too often I hear others say, but Jesus corrected Peter, saying it was his lack of faith, almost making it sound like Peter was embarrassed or ashamed in front of the other disciples. I truly doubt that. I have spent a lot of time on boats in stormy seas. Between the wind blowing and waves slapping the boat, I question if the other disciples still in the boat could even hear Jesus telling Peter, it's your lack of faith.

The point that I wonder about and share is, what about the other disciples just sitting there watching? I'd think at least one would pop up and say; "Hey, that's Peter, Jesus call to me! Let me try." How often is that happening in today's world? Ok maybe not walking on water, but getting up, stepping out of the boat. Taking the risk of failure or humiliation, but taking a few steps, maybe changing the lives of others. How often do people just sit back and say, "Check them out, they're doing so much." Let me tell you, yes a lot has been done through GIBTK, lives changed for generations, but never forget I am not anything special...only a little education and just a willingness to step out of the boat.

To Take A Chance

I wonder what lies deep in your heart? Is there something that keeps coming back up? A nagging to take a chance, a still silent voice saying you can make a difference? May I urge you to take the steps out of the boat.

      After returning from adopting my daughter Kristina, I was haunted by the faces of the many kids I had met in the orphanages, wondering what was their future? I came to the conclusion that I'd rather be called a fool one more time, than miss something that I was called to do. How about you? I'm guessing most, if not all, dream of living a life that will leave a mark. They want to live a life of significance or to leave a legacy. A legacy is what we do that lives past our lives.

Make Room For Other's Visions Within The Culture
You need a place where people can flourish within your vision. When a teammate or someone comes to me with a new idea or program, my first response should be— "WOW!" Rather than, "how does this budget or work?," or ask a plethora of ideas and questions trying and working to deflate this new idea. Instead I need to be looking for others to come up with ideas, ones that are not mine. I need to step back and give myself time to think and process, to bring others in as counsel.

Be open for new ideas and ways from others. As a leader and visionary of GIBTK, I need to remind myself I am not the alpha and omega of this organization, I am but a part. There are many who can come alongside and will have ideas to better the organization and make it stronger. Have additional vision. I must be open. Yes, the initial vision and culture of the organization must be clear, but also leave room for other's dreams.

Giving It Back To Kids had grown to a place that others ideas and even vision could fit under our umbrella. Huong was a funny, OK a "crazy" young lady with a heart of compassion and great English skills. She left GIBTK. I think mostly because of a lack of fulfillment, although I did not know it at the time. She went to other organizations and eventually opened a thriving English School for kids. Although I really had never heard her idea when she was on our team, I'm fairly certain I would have dismissed it by saying, "It is not what GIBTK does or how can it be funded?"

At the writing of this we are paying for a number of our students to attend Huong's English classes. Was she not a fit under our umbrella, or better said a perfect fit under our umbrella! Recently I heard it said the following way. We are called to wake other people's dreams up and to be sure there is room for their dreams within our umbrella whenever possible.

I needed to get comfortable with sharing my struggles and failures because there are others that are feeling the same thing, struggling with the same thing and feel ostracized. That is, of course, unless what you're sharing is going to harm another person. I had to risk being vulnerable. To be myself. I was told early on I'm only as sick as my secrets. Secrets grow in darkness and when light hits them, they disappear. Now I believe this needs to be done wisely.

After some things I've written in this book I stopped and wondered, what will they think and say when they read what I wrote?... but I have not written about my total life. It is not for this place, but rest assured I have found those I can and have shared all the good, the bad and the ugly of my life. What I have experienced is this. When I have the opportunity to be vulnerable, inevitably there are others who hear and think or tell me, "Wow, I thought it was just me that felt that way or did that." Seeing others get vulnerable and honest helped me to do so myself, to be more open and candid, to let others in. One thing I need to be careful of when being candid is not to do so when it might hurt another.

Learn to be present and enjoy every moment, because the next moment it's going to be history and passes quickly. All too often I have spent, or better said wasted, days thinking about what's coming, both exciting things and fearful things. I could be worrying, projecting,dreaming, or spend the day thinking, regretting or reliving a past event. Doing this I was missing what I have right now, the present! I would be reading at times and be thinking of the future or past, only to realize I've finished a couple pages and don't know what I read. I am learning, (yes I said still learning), to be present with friends and acquaintances.

I heard a story some time ago about the difference between a pessimist and an optimist. One young boy saw everything that was good and the other could only see what was wrong. They filled up two separate observation rooms with horse manure. They put a young boy into each room and began to observe. In the first room they saw the young lad acting much like they expected, sitting there showing his displeasure. He was sad, to say the least.

After a time they went on to observe the second young boy sitting in a similar room filled with horse manure. However, this kid was jumping back and forth, up and down, laughing and throwing the horse manure all about! This boy was having a great time! Puzzled, they went into the room and asked what he was doing. The young boy replied, "With all this horse poop, there must be a pony in here somewhere!" So what do we do and how do we act when our lives are filled with so much? Yes, there have been very difficult times of personal and professional challenges in my life. And I work to remind myself about looking for the pony in all this, ...remind myself of the scripture from James, "consider it all joy when trials and tribulations come." To just be in the present.

Character

Character is built on the inside. It is what a person is like in private, what we do when no one is watching. A friend of mine's mentor suggested that he do three things a day for someone else and not tell anyone. So my friend took the suggestion on. The next day he went out and did three things and didn't tell anyone. Then he called his mentor. His mentor asked him; "So how was your day today what's going on?" My friend told him, "I did those three things and here's what I did." His mentor said, "Well you just told somebody, so go back out and do three more things."

Although I know the above lesson, still when I am paying for my food bill at the counter and there's a tip jar, for some reason I more than often wait until the cashier can see me put the money into their jar. What's up with that? Am I doing it for attention or to be recognized? I know I'm being a little tough on myself and maybe you. Character is built most often in your private life. It's one thing to do things and get accolades for it, but another to do it when no one is watching. The way you look outside does matter to an extent, but what really matters is who you are in private.

Character can be defined by action. It is our character that helps define our destiny, or future. Character withstands the test of time and yes it does take time and work to build character. But it is worth every bit of effort.

If I have a choice I'd pick character over talent. This goes for friends, those I choose to spend time with and especially for those we choose to build our team with. Skills can be taught, while character can not! Dr.

Cole always said, "Talent can take you to places your character can't sustain."

How often do we hear of an athlete or an actor, or so many others, that their talents took them to great places, but their character could not sustain it? They built lives or their teams to fame and riches, only to end in disgrace. I hesitate to even write this, to put it into print. My prayer from the beginning has been for God to build my character. In this time and day we hear of so many falls and it's a fear that I have. I hope that my character is close to sustaining what God is building in Giving It Back to Kids. It is one of the reasons that I spend so much time in this book talking about being a learner. And that I still spend time every day, rarely do I miss a day, where I'm not reading something, listening to something, striving to learn not only head knowledge, but stuff that's gonna change my heart, so that my insides can come close to matching my outsides.

An older nice person vs. a mean crabby person, is character. Have you ever met an older person that just seems mean? The kind of person you feel you just don't want to be around for very long? When they speak, most of what they say has an edge or a bite to it. And then I'm sure we've all met and all know an older person who is just a joy to be around. They're loving, kind, encouraging, and happy. You just wanna snuggle up and hug on them. The difference? Why is one person so sweet and another person so crabby?

I remember my spiritual father Ed Cole saying, "As we get older we lose more and more of our personality and charisma. What's left is our character. When we were young we've got "game." We've got personality traits that help us make it through business, through life, make friends in school and after school gets out. But as we get older and older, what's left is character." I'm sure we've heard people say that I'm getting so old that I really don't care what they think. I can just tell them what I think, the truth. Unfortunately, truth from a bitter person might not be so kind, might not be so loving. It might have a natural slant towards negativity. On the other hand there's those whose words are always kind, even when truth is spoken. They can encourage even when correcting you. You walk away feeling love.

As for me, I pray, hope and yes work towards building character the best I can. I laugh when I think of this, everybody's got to be known for something. Way too often I hear people start talking and they mention about me "lovingly," talking about taking shopping carts back to where they belong. Well let's take it a step further. What about taking it back and it's not your shopping cart? Does that bless somebody or make their job a little bit easier? You bet! Think of the worker or the person who finally sees an open parking space, only to see that someone left their shopping cart in it. How about walking down the market aisle and seeing a package that has fallen off the shelf, picking it up and making the stocker's job just a bit easier?

There's so many other ways to build character. A lot of it is backed by service. As I mentioned earlier, character can be defined by action. And often being of service begins where convenience ends.

I look for people who have what I want. Not riches, fame, or a nice house, but rather people with character. Those that treat others with respect and kindness no matter what they're worth. And I ask what do you do? How did you get there? When I see an older person who's kind and loving I want to be a friend to them and just hang out. I ask, "So what did you do, or do you do, to be like you are? How did you do it?" Invariably, somehow they learned to think of others first. I think I want what they have. If I wanna be like that when I get older, it's up to me to build my character.

Friends of mine were told we need to be careful that life is not treated like a buffet table, one where I take what I think I want or need and expect the results that others have that have taken the whole thing; the lessons, the experiences, the disciplines.

Too often in the past I've seen something in others and want that for my own life. It's much like when I've tasted a wonderful cake, sweet, flavorful and just plain delicious. I will ask for the recipe. I look at it and see there's a ton of butter, lots of eggs and sugar. I begin to think too many calories, too much fat, way too much cholesterol! So my keen mind says, "I know! I'll adjust the recipe." I'll cut out most of the butter, substituting the sugar with artificial sweetener, egg beaters for the eggs. Then I will wonder why I ended up with a dry biscuit.

If I want the type of organization others have, or what I see in others, such as their traits and character, friends that I want in my life; it is best to come alongside and learn what they do, then do it too! If you want what others have, do what others do. Of course there are exceptions. Sometimes God may have a different plan or adjustments. But begin with what they did and see what happens. Once you find something that's working, keep doing it! Don't think, ok I got this and go back to the old way of doing things.

Beware Of Being Puffed Up Rather Than Built Up
What this means is be careful not to take the things we learn and use it only as head knowledge, where we look good and sound wise. Rather, let what we learn from them transform us. It is important that I be built up rather than puffed up. That I practice walking in what I learn, before I start preaching or teaching or correcting. That I'm able to live it out rather than preach it.

I once heard a talk about this. The speaker mentioned being in a class and a fellow student stood up and began to quote an entire chapter from the Bible. Awestruck to say the least. But then the thought came, a tape player or in more modern terms, a MP3 player can do that. Someone can memorize the verses, but can they live it out? There is the old adage that children won't always do what you tell them to do, but they always do what they see you do. It is just like the saying I mentioned earlier; that I can't hear what you're saying because your actions are too loud. We can spout all the wisdom and all the knowledge sounds really good, but way too often those we are trying to lead can't hear us. It is puffed up versus built up. As a leader what are others seeing you do? What would others say about how you act?

I wonder how often people don't do the things that God has called them to do because of fear, finances or timing. They say or think; yeah but.... versus you bet! Too often my first response is negative. I've found that often when I do the opposite of what my brain says I end up happier. When I do the things my head says it wants to do, way too often I end up depressed and achieving results that are opposite of what I hoped to attain.

Learn To Take Contrary Actions

First I thought there's only black and white. That there is right and wrong. And yes there is right and wrong. I had to learn that yes there's black and white and there may be grays too. And then came a revelation that way too often there's black AND white. There's times where I meet someone and realize what's "right" for me, may very well not be right for another. What's "right" for another is not necessarily right for me. There are different places of maturity we may be at. As well as differences in culture, which can make a total difference in what's "right."

I remember coming to the realization and learning the facts and the differences in culture between Asia and the Western world. I remember sitting with a friend living in Vietnam. I asked him, "How do you do this? Live and work in this culture without going crazy?" He said, "Robert, don't you understand, Western culture is built on Aristotle logic, Asian culture is built on Confucius logic."

One big example of what might be right for another that may not be right for me is in Vietnam, relationship trumps truth. I could be lying to you, you'll know I'm lying and I know that you know I'm lying and we will walk away best friends. I've asked many Vietnamese friends about this and they look at me like, well yeah! Of course! Almost even saying, "What a silly question."

I remember clearly one day I was visiting Universal Studios with a friend's son. He was in his final year at a University in the US. I asked him the question, is relationship more important than truth and repeated what I said above. He looked at me and said, "Well yes, relationships are more important than the truth!" I remember the exact spot we were at and he took a few more steps ahead of me, turned around and looked at me puzzled and said, "It's the same here in the United States, right?" I looked at him and said, "No, in the United States if there's dishonesty, it's a relationship breaker." He turned and walked away shaking his head, totally puzzled. Please remember he had been living in the US for 4 years at that time. As I work with different cultures I need to always keep in mind there's black, white, there's gray and there's black AND white.

Different people are at different levels of maturity, so we need to be careful not to hold them responsible for the level that we are at. As I have grown and dare I say matured, I seem to also raise the bar for how other people are to act and their level of maturity. I often used to say, "I'm a quick learner, but a quicker forgetter." Ha Ha! It seems as though I may have had it all wrong. I'm seeing at this point in my life, that I in fact, am a slow learner. I so often need to remind myself that I need to let others be who they are at that time of their life. It took me many years to begin to have a slight bit of clarity in my own life, so why do I not allow others to have the same time too?

I have often told a story I heard from a Pastor. The ending is that God loves me just as I am, but loves me way too much to leave me there. I share that with our GIBTK team often, so often they finish the story in unison, saying "You love us just as we are, but love us too much to leave us there."

There's another story of the hula hoop where we imagine an invisible hula hoop around us. We are responsible for what's inside of the hula hoop and not what's outside. Some might say, "But wasn't Vietnam far outside of your hula hoop?" Yes, but no. My hula hoop was extended to enclose much more as time went on. God saw us as we worked, saw faithfulness (yes lots of mistakes, but correction attempts) and grew what was inside our hoops. But I still need to allow others to be where they're at, at that time. I guess it may be as simple as a matter of judgement? Or a thought just came to me. I'm typing on a plane in too tight seats. I had my legs crossed, the man in front of me brought his seat back. I struggled to unfold my legs, now typing squeezed tight. I was looking at the back of his head, thinking not so kind thoughts. My first thought is, well I'll tilt my seat back. Then it hits me, maybe learn from this guy, stay within my hula hoop, be kind to the person behind me. Humm, yes it can be uncomfortable for us to take steps that help us to grow and make changes in our life.

Maturity Has Nothing To Do With Age

Dr. Edwin Louis Cole shared one day that maturity has nothing to do with age, but acceptance of responsibility. How often do we see a grown man or woman that acts as a child? Or a young child or teen that acts as an adult because they show an acceptance of their responsibilities. Maturity comes with the acceptance of responsibility. The more mature you are, the more we begin to accept responsibility for others as well. Dr. Cole taught that Christlikeness and manhood or womanhood are synonymous. If that be the case and I believe it is, then our example of how to live or maybe better said our goal, is to live as Christ did. Think for a moment, what did Christ do? He accepted responsibility for not only his stuff, but all of ours!

Always be quick to see where I am wrong or what my part of it is. The greater the maturity the more responsibilities we take on. I once saw this lovely young lady in a car next to me. She had a license plate frame that said, so many many boys and so few men. Unfortunately I'm speaking to the males who are reading. Dr Coles often taught me that being a male is a matter of birth. Being a man is a matter of choice. A man accepts responsibility. He does not blame and offer excuses. Too often I've heard women complain that their husband acts like she's their mother. That's way too true of some males. They get married and really are looking for a mother to take care of their needs.

In leadership, in home, work and organizations, a mature leader does not blame his team. He does not make excuses when things go awry. He accepts responsibility. It is his fault. If the company or organization is "not behaving," perhaps the first place to look is at himself. Same with family. How a family, company or organization runs or "looks" is a good sign of what the lead person is like. I've heard it said that the characteristics of the family or company originate with the leader.

Say what you mean, mean what you say and do what you say. This single sentence has been a key to my growth in many ways. When I talk about this to others I often use the following example. "I really want to give you a million dollars and I really mean it. But if I do not do it, it is a lie!" A half truth is a full lie. I was taught that a man is only as good as his word. If I tell someone I'll be there at 6 but get there at 6:15, what is that? I lied! I need to make amends. Way too often the fall back excuse is there was unexpected traffic, when the truth is I should have left earlier.

Dr. Cole often said, "You can judge a man's or woman's character by how well they keep their word. Our word is our bond." I truly think that a key part of the growth of GIBTK was due to this. We did not say we're going to do something and then did not do it. There were many times officials would urge us to "say" we would do something more than we could commit to. They'd say it's ok if we can't, but say you can so we can put it on our report. We as an organization said what we meant, meant what we said and then did what we said.

I can't hear what you're saying because your actions are too loud. To be honest, the first place I saw this was on the wall of my probation officer. But it stuck with me. For me it means I must "strive" to show what I believe by my actions, rather than say one thing while my behavior shows differently. At one point I went to our GIBTK team and asked, "If GIBTK says one of our core beliefs or values is relationships, what are we doing to walk this out? Are we being relational? Do our actions show we care?" Or I've had to personalize it. I say I love my family, but had to begin to ask myself, "What do I put in front of them?" With the GIBTK team and my life the question is; can someone hear what we say by our actions? We all heard kids won't always do what we tell them, but they'll do what they see us do.

Learn From Others

Learn to ask others what they learned from their successes and their failures and adapt those lessons to my life where appropriate. Life lessons are key to me. It is the reason I'm writing this book. I heard John Maxwell speak one time on this matter. He suggested asking friends and those we look up to what lessons they have learned in life, what have they learned from their mistakes and also added, do you know anyone that I should know?

For me, I have to be careful for several reasons. The first is if it is something sensitive, my first reaction is not me! I'm not like that. Too often I look for how I'm different. Early on I was taught to look for similarities, rather than differences. Once I do this there is a great opportunity for me to learn or pick up "hints" to living life through others' life lessons.

The second thing I need to be careful of, even in how I word this. When I first heard him say "Who do you know that I should know," it hit me a bit off. It felt like networking. Using others to get what I need, or more what I think I want. Then one day I was having dinner with a friend. He was a high level official in the Vietnamese government who had met four of our US presidents. I asked him what he has learned in life, from successes and from failures. His answer was sincerity. Where our insides match our outside. He had recently retired and it was then that it hit me. Perhaps he knew someone who I should know as well and asked. Indeed he did. Doing so to this day for me has not been easy, but it's not about me; rather it's about GIBTK, transforming a nation/region and changing the unhealthy parts of culture.

God could put something to do on someone's heart that is such a big thing. It could be a huge vision and dream. They get excited. Then get caught up in the what, how, when of the huge thing and settle for doing a good deed, adopting a puppy from a shelter, instead of doing what God has called them to do. Please understand, adopting a puppy is noble, but was there a possibility of doing something larger in addition to adopting the puppy? You don't want to miss a larger calling.

One of my mentors often said, "To goodness and kindness we make promises, but to pain we become obedient." His mentor taught him that pain may very well be a gift from God. It's the only thing sharp enough to cut through our egos. I have added that the amount of pain we're in, is directly proportional to our resistance to growth or change. So often I see my loved ones, my friends and those I pass by, thinking if I could just say something to them, help them to see, they would miss the struggles. But just for today I remind myself to let others have the dignity to make their own mistakes, to learn at their own pace. I need to mind my own business and unless asked, to keep my opinion or my ideas to myself. Of course, there are situations that do need us to step up and say something.

Too often I look to please myself or to make myself feel good. I can use things like food, shopping, cigars or sex. All those are good except in certain situations, except for maybe the cigars. However, when I'm using them to fix myself, or to fill a void I may be feeling, it's a deterrent from learning to be just where I am today and being aware in the moment.

These side things can mask where I am at, only for a short time. The real feelings are still there. I'm feeling lonely so I go online and shop. Makes me ok for a moment, but this passes and I still feel lonely. Instead I should be reaching out to someone, making a call with what sometimes feels like a ten ton phone. My thoughts say, "but I don't want to bother them." What I keep "relearning" is that others most often feel the same. They don't want to reach out, yet crave relationships.

I was once told to call this man regularly. He told me, "Just call and tell me you're practicing making my phone call." I've been known to tell others, "Just call me and say I'm practicing making my phone call." What happens is a relationship is built. It is just a simple sentence, but so many times I'd get that simple call and could hear that their voice sounded "different." The practice call turned into a 20-30 minute call. Please know that I'm not the "social" type. For myself, I have had to learn contrary actions. Way too often my ideas were not the best ideas. I had to build a fence of people around me that I had relationships with. When things got tough, crazy or decisions needed to be made, I have those friends that are current with my life. They know me, how I think and I could call and not need to spend 30 minutes catching them up. Usually the catching up was not clear, but slanted towards the mood I was in.

You Bet, Versus Yeah But

I heard it put this way, sheep say "you bet" and goats say "yeah but." Sheep follow shepards, goats, well they go their own way. Yes leaders lead but they aren't the soloist that goats are.

Too often my first reaction when asked to do something out of my way, or out of my comfort zone is negative. I have trained myself to say "you bet!" rather than "yeah but".... "gosh I'd be happy to help but..." I give my first answer of "you bet" and then figure it out, figure out how I'll make time or make a plan, or how you can do it.

Yes there are times I've said you bet and not been able to do it. You might say, but your word is your bond, you wrote that earlier. True, but when unable to complete what I said I would do, I go back to the person and say "I'm sorry I can't help, please forgive me?" And often I add, "what can I do to make it right?"

Don't Go Into Your Head Alone...

Friends used to say that to me, and add it's a rough neighborhood. This is a line that honestly is tough for me. It's a challenge for me not to fall into the,"he said then I said." Or begin to look at negative feelings, emotions, fear etc. and make them the topic of my head. I often refer to the many thoughts as my committee, which invariably leads to more negative feelings, fears and emotions. So how do I deal with this? I let others in on what I'm thinking. I seek out and build friends I trust. When my head says sit home alone, I call someone and I work to get out.

Another tool I use is journaling, not caring how it sounds or if it's grammatically correct. I have even used words that might not be kind, just to get the feelings and negative thoughts out. I do also work to end with positive things. A gratitude list. We all have something to be grateful for. For me it can start with I can see, I can walk, I have a roof to sleep under. There is a saying that says, "Grateful people are happy people and those that aren't, aren't !"

I've also learned and need to remind myself that what I focus on grows larger, bigger! I need to be careful with where I allow my focus to be. Is it a solution, or is it just thinking of the problem? I know this may be a bit inappropriate, so please forgive me? I often make a comparison of focusing on our problems and sitting in a poopy diaper. I think of an infant that needs their diaper changed and how so often makes a fuss when someone goes to change the diaper. They would rather sit in their dirty diaper warm, comfortable, and end up with a diaper rash.

So it is when we sit in our problems. We focus our attention on the negative and we end up with diaper rash. It is taking contrary actions. I need to look to the solution, finding people that will give positive perspectives, rather than agreeing with me and saying, "you're right, that's so bad." One thing for sure is, it's easier if I let other people into my life that I have a relationship with and can share openly with, when those tough times come up and they surely will.

Too often I look to make myself feel good to be happy, by going for the spectacular and the supernatural. I overshoot the mark. I've realized that way too often my idea of "happy" is not real. My happiness, my contentment is often found in a simple walk in nature, over a cup of coffee with a friend or spending time with family.

The people I choose to have as friends and to be around will help to determine my destiny. Birds of a feather flock together. I need to always remind myself to seek out those that are a little above my pay grade, those that will challenge me and my lifestyle. Whether it be an education, the way I eat or dare I put into words, regular exercise.

My circle of friends are those I choose to be around. When I am with those that are making healthy eating choices, I find myself eating more healthy. If everybody else is ordering healthy dinners at a restaurant I probably will shy away from something that's, how should I say it, "comfort food." I've got men in my life that exercise regularly and to be honest, sometimes I look at some of these guys and their bodies and get angry. But having them in my life gets me back into the gym on a regular basis.

I need to take care of myself, mind, body and spirit. My guys who are readers are constantly reading and recommending books that I must read. I find myself pressing to find reading materials that will grow me personally and professionally, that will help me to understand why I "tick the way I tick" and what keeps me from the things that life has for us. I need to find insight into my leading, staying current with the needs of those I lead, as well as the community I've chosen to lead.

Boundaries

We need to be aware of them, both our own as well as those of others. Boundaries are essential to have and maintain. We need to be careful of having too rigid boundaries. If boundaries are too rigid, they become crystallized with no bend to them at all. They are apt to break if pushed on. It is very important that we do have boundaries, but they can also be flexible. Sometimes they need to bend in a little bit or bend out.

As an example I often show my team a glass plate and a paper plate. I say here's a rigid boundary in the glass plate and then I hit it with a hammer and the plate shatters. Then I hold the paper plate and say, "it still retains its form but I can bend it. Which do you want to be, bendable to situations or so rigid and fixed that when push comes to shove you break?"

Once we do have boundaries we know where to draw the line so to speak and that "no" is a complete answer. There are so many good things to do. There are things that are Godly and make a difference, but we need to learn to say no. We are unable to do everything or we will run out of energy and get burned out.

To Be Aware of Lookie-loos and Hanger-oners

One of my biggest struggles is trying to decipher who to bring to our homes in Vietnam and Cambodia. Our motto was and has been "come and see." I feel my secondary vision and passion is to help others to identify a vision or flame burning within their own hearts. To come alongside them and help any tiny flame within them to become a burning fire, which will lead others to find their purpose. I invited and encouraged all to "come and see," but began to realize that some come to see the "poor kids," to "help" them. They mean no harm, but they enjoy taking kids' photos. So, it is a photo-op so to speak. And later to be able to post on social media and tell friends what they did on their vacations.

I know this sounds harsh and may well be. I forever will remember seeing a poster at the office of an organization working in Cambodia. It showed a child in a cage, being presented on a table, with adults taking photos. Honestly, it breaks my heart to think, what if kids in our homes or programs would or could ever feel this way. I remind myself that the kids in our homes are not in a "zoo," where well meaning tourists who are coming to "help," come and see. I've had some people get upset and say things like, we want to come and see and then we will leave some money. My answer, "Thanks, but can you imagine if you're at home with your family and a van or bus pulls up, strangers come walking in and begin taking selfies and photos throughout your house, seeing your bathrooms, where you sleep, looking in drawers to see what you wear etc.? What would the disruption do to your kids?"

Today we try to distinguish and limit who can come and see. Often we look to see what the guest is bringing. When I say this, I don't necessarily mean funding, but more do they have something to add to the lives of our kids. Recently we have had guests who came and had kids make vision boards. The kids cut photos out of magazines that show their dreams. Then they paste them on a board so they can have visual reminders of their personal dreams and goals.

Others have come to train students how to shake hands and how to act when going to apply for work. Another taught on entrepreneurship. They have asked our college kids to make business plans, etc. and even gave a small cash reward for the best "thought through" ones.

Direct and Clear Communication

Clear communication takes word, gesture and spirit. In Asian culture the communication is generally indirect. I've heard it said, "you have to read the air." For my office staff I explained that I understand that in the Vietnam culture indirect communication is the norm. However, in our work, especially in the office, we have to be very direct in our communication. If it be by emails, text or phone it has to be very direct so there's no misunderstanding.

I've held a bottle of water up in front of our team and said this is a bottle of water. It doesn't mean that I want a cup to pour it in, or there's something wrong with the water, or that I want more water. Those would all be assuming what I mean. If I say here's a bottle of water, that's all I mean. This is a bottle of water. We've adapted this, "Say what you mean, and mean what you say."

As an example I give to the importance of direct and clear communication I use our heart program, or any other urgent matter. Say there is a problem that needs approval from me. The staff would email me. Know that there is a 14 hour time difference between Vietnam and California. They email in the afternoon, Vietnam time. I read it in the morning (one day later due to time change), California time. It's unclear what is being asked because they are using indirect communication. I then email back a question in California daytime, Vietnam's late night, asking for clarity. Another day goes by. They answer in their afternoon which I see when I wake up and answer back. It can be 2-3 or more days if all goes well. In that time an urgent need like a heart surgery can be missed and or too late and a child dies.

I know the above may sound extreme, but it can happen. All could have been avoided with clear, direct communication. I have talked to many government officials working in Vietnam and they all say the same thing. There is so much confusion and mistakes because of indirect communication. With indirect communication we must assume what the other person is saying or asking. For our organization it is vital that we have clear, direct and in time communication.

Looking For The "More"

I tend to beat myself up, always looking for more. If I just did this more or if I just look this way, then I'd be happy. If I had one more suit... instead of living unsatisfied. I have learned and keep reminding myself to accept who I am, where I am and that God loves me just the way I am. I have a tendency to think if I was thinner, if I had more money, more education, then I'd be happy. Truth is this moment is what I have. Learn to enjoy the moments as they pass too quickly. This is as good as it gets right now, so best enjoy the moment!

This also transfers into my spiritual life way too often. I'm sure I'll have push back from readers on my next statement. I fully understand that scripture says we are to learn more about God. I do totally agree to keep growing, maturing, going from newborn to adulthood. But too often I am looking for the next big spiritual revelation. And I have written in this book to be learners, always learning, always seeking to gain wisdom, looking for the next mountain top experience. However I feel that the same principle applies here. It is learning to stay and enjoy the moment the best I can. Sure I keep looking to grow, but moments pass too quickly and become history.

I'm reminded of a time I went to do a nature walk with God. I had my pocket Bible, a notepad and pen in hand. I was going to spend meaningful time with God, to hear and learn from His Word. This day I had decided to walk in the back Bay Area of Newport Beach, California. It happened to be a beautiful spring morning. I began my walk, then noticed all the beauty of the spring flowers blooming. I'd pull myself back and say this is time to learn and hear from God. Walk a bit more and mallard ducks would come flying by, their reflections in the bay water would glisten with beauty. Again I'd pull myself back hoping to reach the next pentacle of God and growth, only to see butterflies flying around.

Next thing I knew my time for my "God walk" was past. As I walked back to my car, I began apologizing to God for missing this time of prayer. Then I felt as though I heard a "God whisper." I felt as though He was asking if I would rather one of my kids kept asking me questions and giving me a list of things they wanted me to do, or would I rather walk with them and they told me about the beauty they saw during our walk? The answer was simple. I know what my kids need, but to hear them enjoying the beauty that is so often around us would be better.

Surely there is time for us to read, learn and pray, but perhaps just enjoying time with God may be something He enjoys more? Sometimes I feel we complicate our relationships with God, but not only God. Perhaps also we do so with those we know closely and those all around us as well. I often need to remind myself to enjoy the moment.

Keep God's Perspective On Current Situation

Too often we get caught up in the "weeds." Some say, "We're so in the middle of it, we can't see the forest from the trees." I heard a story of a man walking into an office. A plaque read, "keep looking down." He asked the person behind the desk, "Shouldn't it be the opposite, keep looking up?" That person surprised him with their answer. They said "No, it's correct. Keep looking down. Keep God's perspective on life and situations. You see God can see where we began, where we are and where He's taking us."

I also remember in the early years walking on the beach where I used to spend a lot of time and still do, seeking God, thanking and praying about GIBTK. This morning I was particularly excited and was just about shouting out loud to God about protecting the kids in Vietnam, that they might fulfill their destiny in God. I was looking for new ways to make a difference in their lives and then...it was like I had this inside quiet voice, a gentle whisper, maybe a God whisper? I heard, "What about the two kids you have at home? What about the wife you have at home?" I realized one more time I was so mission minded, to get things done in Southeast Asia, I was forgetting to take care of the first things, my own family.

Leaders

Good leaders are not the beat on the table type, but rather the set the table type. Too often CEOs are beat on the table types. They come in like a burning hot fire. Problem is they run out of fuel and flame out. Yes things can get done, and for sure I have more often than not fallen to pounding on the table or more, in my case, "jumping up and down". Problem is you scare and or intimidate those you're trying to lead. I wanted to say those on the leader's team, but really wonder if the beat on the table leader is really a leader of "the team." A good leader "sets the table" for his team, earns their respect, gets them to join the vision willingly, to follow rather than be pushed. I believe this type of leadership inspires others to want to follow and become leaders themselves. For GIBTK this has often been the case.

With newer leaders the problem is, there are mistakes made. But I often share with those on our team, if you/we are not making mistakes, then we are not trying anything new. We are not innovators. We will lose the lead and become followers to other organizations. This is not necessarily a bad thing. However for us, we like finding new ways to meet new challenges and always growing needs and issues.

Service Has Been and Is Our Culture

We often say that we are able to lead only to the degree we are willing to serve. It begins at the top. My spiritual father, Ed Cole, always used to say the characteristics of the kingdom emanate from the top. You can walk into a company or organization and see what the boss is like, as his characteristics will be throughout the organization.

This is a lesson that I have to keep teaching and reminding myself. Or more importantly or correctly said, that I have to implement. One of my big regrets was one time when we had a Tet store. Tet is the lunar new year in Vietnam. It is custom to buy new things for the family. We host a "Tet store" where the poor families of the community can purchase items at highly reduced cost. The team showed up hours before it was to open, moving the goodies from our office to a few doors down to the restaurant where we were holding the event. I was in town that day and yes I chose to stay in the hotel room, thinking the team has this. If I were true to my words, I would've been there and helped to set up.

What really made it sting was a friend of mine from Australia was there representing a very large Church from the Chicago area. He was there talking to us about leadership conferences. A VIP, he and his wife woke early to help my staff to move the supplies. I need to be willing and make myself remember to put into action, that service has to be the key and it must start with me if I have any hopes of the organization I get to lead of having that characteristic. I need to be willing to help clean, move chairs or whatever comes up.

The old saying comes to mind again, "People might not always do what you tell them, but they're more likely to do the things that they see you do." This is especially true when they see what their leader does. I have to think about what I do want my emerging leaders to model. Is it what I model or not?

Don't Let Others Create Your World...

They will make it too small. When I first began GIBTK I was told we would never last. That it couldn't be done that way, or it's too much work! I am so glad that God places a bit of something in me that when I hear, "can't be done," it inspires me and I just gotta get it done.

For us it was that we wanted to stay in contact and in relationship with those we helped, for it not to be a one time deal or as some like to call it, a "photo op." To be fair and honest, I realize that there are different callings in life. There are real times when relief work is needed to meet the immediate needs. Then there is the development type of work. That is what I felt God had called Giving It Back To Kids to do. Yes there are many times that we have come along and met immediate needs. However, whenever possible we have tried to stay in contact.

Yes this is a huge amount of extra work, especially as GIBTK continues to grow and add numbers to our work. There were more and more people to try and stay in contact with. I asked that every team member spend, or better said invest, 60 minutes every work day reaching out to past recipients. Some really didn't want to hear from us, but others sure did! We hear stories that encourage us to keep doing what we do. Other times we hear of another way to help someone walk to the next step in their lives.

My point in having said all this is to do what your heart says to you. Just try it! Hey you might fall short, but don't let others create your world for you. Yes, listen to others for guidance and wisdom, but go the route in your heart. Be smart, but take a chance and who knows, you might just do as Steve Jobs once said to his team at Apple, "Go dent the universe."

Trust

To trust we need to trust, but verify. Trust is something that did not or does not come easy to me. So often I would say, "You have to earn my trust!" Then I got to thinking one day, how can someone earn my trust if I don't begin to trust them first? Yes I had to begin to first trust people, giving them the opportunity. Looking back there've been times where I was hurt, disappointed and taken advantage of. But honestly there's been more benefit for myself and for the organization from trusting others, from letting go and delegating.

As far as leading the organization, I had to learn to delegate. Yes, inspect what I expected. At one point I remember hearing a friend share about training and delegating. He used this example of a golf instructor. First the instructor will say, "Watch me as I take a golf swing." Then the instructor would continue explaining. Next you try putting the golf club into the student's hands, while the instructor helps to guide with his own hands over the student's hands. Together they would take the golf swing. Next the instructor would step back and say, "OK, now you take a swing alone and I will watch."

So it has been with much of the growth of Giving It Back To Kids. I had to learn to trust others and to let go of things. I'd think it would be so much faster if I just did it myself. I needed to get away from the old saying, if you want it done right, better do it yourself! I recognized there was no way to grow if I kept it all in my own hands.

One day I clearly remember walking on the beach in prayer and meditation and there were a lot of seashells on the beach. I began to pick them up and before long there were more than I could hold in my hand. Then the thought came to me, that this is the way it is with Giving It Back To Kids, there's more than I can hold in my own hand. So I began to train others and to step back and watch them do. There's always going to be mistakes. I tell my team if we're not making mistakes we're not trying anything new. But I also tell them, please don't make big mistakes and let's not make the same mistake over and over.

Time- Respect The Clock

Begin on time and end on time. If we begin late that means we will reward the people who were late and punish those that came on time. In many cultures, especially Vietnam, they call it "rubber time". That's when the time for a meeting to start is given. It is just a rough idea of the start. Often if a meeting or even a wedding is supposed to start at 1, people will begin getting ready at 1 to go to the meeting, wedding or event. I know it sounds crazy in much of western culture. You might think, oh Robert's speaking rhetorically, but there's truth to it.

Another lesson I also have learned is that when given a certain amount of time to speak, to respect the time given. Say what needs to be said in the time you are given.

Cultural Differences and The Need To Be Aware

One of the biggest and on the top of the lessons I've learned list, is about culture. Each culture whether from the US, Vietnam or any other region or country, are different. It doesn't make one right over the other. However I want to challenge you to think about this. Can the challenge or argument be made that even in one country the culture can be different? For instance can the culture be different when we are in the city and in some ways very different in the villages in the countryside? Which one is right? Both are.

One of the lessons I learned is how we work within the cultures. Can culture be different in different families? When you're with one family you act a certain way, when you're with another family you have to act differently. How about the culture of a healthy person and a disabled person? Or what about the family of a disabled person versus a healthy person's family?

We may be correct when we say, "transforming unhealthy culture is part of GIBTKS quest." However before we can do that we have to look at other people's culture, try to understand it and change our methods and thinking, before we can work to transform something to a healthier culture.

I know some may ask what do I mean by unhealthy culture? There are some cultures in the mountainous areas that believe that if a mother dies while giving birth they need to bury the newborn infant alive with the mother. Or if she dies while breastfeeding they bury the infant alive with the mom. I've read a number of accounts of people walking through cemeteries and hearing babies, buried and crying. Also, in some cultures selling your child is normal.

Another time I was at a devoted missionaries school in Southeast Asia. The country is known for its human trafficking. GIBTK had helped fund completion of the school. One of the floors of the building was to train pastors. The school was built inside a former children's brothel. It was creepy that they had all these little small rooms. I couldn't even begin to think about what had happened in those rooms.

There was an area that was open, somewhat of a patio with a wall that was from the building next door. The missionary leaned against the wall and told me that this is still a brothel.

I asked if it was a CHILDREN'S brothel? He said, "No they're all older." I asked how old? What I heard next angered me, broke my heart, amazed me! He replied, "Well, they're 14 or 15 years old." I looked at him, aghast at what I just heard and said, "Those are children!" His answer to this day haunts me. He said, "What are you gonna do, it's the culture." The culture must change.

Culture is what sets up our guidelines for living. If we come in and begin to tell others how they should live their lives and it goes against their culture, their minds close, as does their cooperation and willingness to change. They don't care how much we know, until they know how much we care.

What if we can reach in and accept them as they are, in their culture? Then it can open their minds and hearts. When they feel unaccepted by us they will close off their hearts and minds and build up defenses. They will feel rejected and can become not only defensive, but offensive as well. Acceptance is not the same as approval. Acceptance simply means that we validate them for where they are at, we acknowledge their current situation. I once heard someone say, "God loves us just the way we are, but loves us too much to leave us that way."

In the earlier years of GIBTK, government officials called me California short pants. They would ask my staff, "when is Mr. California short pants coming back?" You see I wore short pants everywhere I went. It was hot and humid and hey, I'm from California. Makes sense right? Then one day I was at a wheelchair distribution outside of Hanoi. We were giving away 300 wheelchairs that day. As people were gathering I watched. This man came up to me, clearly drunk, almost falling over. He looked at me with disdain. Pointed at my short pants and my bare legs and wagged his finger at me while shaking his head. To be honest my first impression and my first thoughts were, clearly you don't know who you're talking to! You'll see when I get up in front of the stage and speak to everybody. Then you'll show me the respect I deserve. I can be such a fool, LOL.

Not long after it became clear to me that I was going against the culture. That it was not normal for people to wear short pants in public, much less at official events. That I was closing off minds. Though I might have something important to say, they clearly were watching through the filter of disdain and really wouldn't hear what I had to say. If we don't fit the culture of the people we're talking to, you create breaks or hindrances in their acceptance to new ideas.

One of the opportunities GIBTK has had is to bring leadership training to Vietnam, particularly to the churches. There is a leadership conference held yearly in the United States. They asked us to bring the conference to Vietnam via high quality videos, using venues that can facilitate a wow effect. Part of what we do requires needing to go to the conference in person and decide which speakers would best fit the culture and are the most needed messages in Vietnam. Representatives from all the other countries would gather together after the conference and decide which speakers would be most appropriate for their cultural setting.

One speaker came out and had a great message, it was just perfect for SE Asia. Unfortunately, he too was another Californian and he was wearing flip-flops. Those of us that were representing Asian cultural nations all agreed that he would not be acceptable, not because of his message, but because of the shoes or the sandals he chose to wear. We need to be careful as we walk into different cultures of how we behave or can be perceived, in order to set up the best atmosphere for others to hear the message we're bringing. This is the same if it is with a neighbor, in-laws or nations. There are definitely times that we must stand for what we believe or for what is right.

When I first came to Vietnam I felt like we needed to come in like a giant fireworks show that as many as possible can see and remember. To be clear, my usual style or what I am most comfortable with, is to stay in the background or in the back of a room and watch people enjoy something that I may have funded, not getting any attention. Entering into Vietnam I felt as though we needed to have the wow effect. Wow effect is what we like to call it when you walk into a room or see something and your first thought is wow! I felt as though when someone came across GIBTK it needed to be memorable.

We've all had that experience where we see something new and the first thought that comes to our mind is wow! I'm sure as you read this you can think back and there's probably several things that pop right up in your memory of seeing or experiencing that left the wow impression. I certainly can.

I know this is not for everybody starting an organization, but for us we had to go in there and get attention, make a big splash so to speak. To be memorable!

I want to be careful here in saying that I didn't look to get attention for myself, but rather for the organization. Whenever possible then and even today, in fact even more so today, it is our team that gets the attention. For us the wow effect has worked well, whether it be in our work or in our yearly fundraiser. We work hard to make the room have the wow effect. I know some may think, but my vision is in countries or places that we can be imprisoned or worse for what we do. True, and I surely do know. GIBTK being in a communist nation and being a Christian based organization, I certainly understand. We sought and still seek wisdom.

Hill Top Versus Valley

Too often we seek the mountaintop experiences, a glorious view looking down upon everything. Yet when we get to the valley we feel differently. We see all the giant bugs and roots that are tripping us up. The plants that have giant thorns are ripping and tearing at our flesh. So it is with life and has been in leading GIBTK. We get to these high points and we want to live there. That's not the way it is. The valley is where most people live, where the organizations we lead are most of the time, not on the mountaintops. It's in the valley that the greatest work is done. This is where fields are planted and harvested. Yes there are problems and issues and stuff happens.

I've looked at friends and said, "Why does it have to be so hard?" But it's in that hardness, the tough times, that the real work is done, that lives are transformed. Even the road down to the valley will first look like a quaint little winding road when looking down from the mountain top. When we get on it, we realize that it's full of bumps and curves and dangerous cliffs to fall off of.

I was walking on the beach again and I was looking for a revelation from God, another mountaintop experience if I was to be real. And it hit me that instead of just reaching up looking for that emotional and spiritual high, why didn't I just enjoy the beach and God's creations. Just walk and love life. Live in the moment instead of always reaching for the high points, for that special moment, for that revelation of the mountaintop experience.

The Summit experience does give us beautiful vision. It is inspirational, but climbing up to that summit is not easy. It is challenging. Going down is fraught with danger as well, filled with slippery rocks. There are places that a seemingly safe trail turns into landslides. It is often in these "summit" experiences that our vision grows. From the high points we can see further if we look. Just remember we must descend from the mountain tops or the summits and re-enter everyday life. The key for me is to not live off the summit experiences and to keep trudging down the road looking how best to lead others to the vision we saw, the next level of growth.

Modern thinking says define your strengths and build on those. There's a lot of truth in that and I certainly believe we need to know our strengths and strengthen them. But I go back to a place in the Bible where it says, "In your weaknesses I am made strong." Surround yourself with people that are smarter than you or more gifted and talented. For sure find those who are strong in the areas of your weaknesses.

With GIBTK we have done just that. Often we first look for those with character and desire to learn. We look to discover their gifts, talents or strengths. Another point is evolution versus revolution. As our organization continues to grow I often mention this. It is important to always try to carefully work to keep the initial vision and culture of GIBTK intact. Bring or hire on your team those who are smarter, more intelligent, gifted or talented than you, but willing to learn, not know-it-alls.

At this point I hate to even type the next thing out. I personally am a bit weary of "experts." For GIBTK we began and continue to do things a bit differently than most other organizations and from the beginning many said we would not last. Well it's been 18 years as of this writing. When we have had experts come along they have had a way they have "always" done it or how "everyone" does it. If they are teachable, great. If they are set in their ways, I would rather avoid the conflicts. At this time in GIBTK we are entering a new level. We have brought new members on the board, some with great experience in other organizations. However, they understand it's best to walk alongside and learn, bringing their experience as needed.

I'm reminded of something I heard Colin Powel speak on once. He shared that as a general he liked it when those below him would come up with a "better plan." He'd want them to fight for their idea like their life depended on it. However, if he as the general made his decision, he expected them to fall in line and be in agreement with his decisions and leadership. If they still felt strongly he'd want them to gather more information, then come back and try to convince him. But during the other times they needed to be in agreement and be in line with what was going on in the organization. I also heard it said this way, "agreement is the place of power."

Bribes

From the beginning we decided not to bribe. I've had many other organizations working in the same area tell us, you have to. We have not. I'm sure there's been times where I was tempted. I remember one time a container of wheelchairs had arrived at customs. We received containers regularly, but for some reason this one was held up. The donor organization was Free Wheelchair Mission and they had a team of donors arriving to be part of the distribution within a week. Customs was asking for a "special" fee (read bribe) which was the equivalent to about $70 USD. I told Tam, our Southeast Asia Director, just pay it! She looked straight into my eyes and said, "No we will not pay a bribe! We will sit and wait until they get tired of us and release the container, don't worry." And we did wait a few days and the customs office finally did release it.

There was another time in a country bordering Vietnam we were just looking to expand into. We were trying to get our license from the government to work there legally. I had met one of the head of states and he referred me to his assistant to process the paperwork.

Finally after a month or two we went into the assistant's office, after all the required paperwork had already been sent to him. He smiled very kindly and said, "Yes the paperwork is filed properly." And he continued, "with the person you know being a high level official, it could be done today or it could sit on this computer for three years." He went on to say that "many NGO's also provide us gifts, like cars, motorbikes or even computer systems." We thanked him, got up and walked out. I looked at the friend I had with me and she asked, "Did he just ask for a car?" I replied, "he sure did!" Long story short is it took three years, but we never provided a bribe.

The amazing thing about that story is that the same assistant became an ally of ours. He began to help us in other areas without ever mentioning a bribe. I remember talking to one of my board members about it and wondering what changed with that guy? And we decided that perhaps it was that we weren't like so many other organizations, that we had integrity and we are willing to wait!

I was speaking with a businessman the other day, an owner and leader of a large company on the subject of gifts or bribes. He has many salesmen and says that often it's expected for them to buy gifts, lunches, dinners etc. He said they have begun to follow two rules. The first one is easy, is it legal? The second one I just loved. Would the boss of the person we're talking to approve of the gift we are giving?

What brought on the conversation is I mentioned that sometimes we give a small gift. Often I have brought a box of chocolate from the US to an official's wife. Or on times that officials have come to California with their children, I'll take them to Disneyland or something similar. But when it comes to giving a bribe to get something done, we take the hard stand not to. It is difficult at times, because we want to get something done. In fact at the time of this writing we are waiting on paperwork for a container of medical equipment we've had stuck in customs for over six weeks. We are just waiting to get the paperwork to open the container and retrieve the goods. Trust me, I am tempted to ask, how much do they want? But we must take the difficult way and wait.

Mission Or Vision Trips

So often I found, especially with western mentality, that visitors want to go and build something or to do something physical. And I understand the spirit and the heart behind it. However, for countries like Vietnam we have found it's not the wisest thing. I read in the book Toxic Charity about a church, I believe in Mexico, that gets painted six times a year by well meaning "short term" missionaries. The hope of the church was that when they leave, they would have left something they can really use.

This really came home to me when we had a group of veterans who came on a trip to Vietnam. They wanted to build wheelchairs for the disabled, asking us to prepare 40 chairs for them to assemble and distribute. Sounded great. Unfortunately because of the heat, their age and fitness, they were only able to assemble about 12. My team and I assembled the rest.

It dawned on me that we have an agreement with our government partners that we get the chairs to port. Our government partners are responsible for customs clearance, waiving of these and duties, transportation, storage and assembly. They hire day laborers to assemble the chairs. So basically this well-meaning mission trip hurt the local economy. In Vietnam as in many countries, labor is really cheap. May I suggest that you consider what is the effect of your short-term mission trip? Perhaps begin thinking of them as vision trips, exposing others to see things and touch their hearts in places they didn't know existed.

Another way we strive, though not perfectly, is to try to help the local business community. If at all possible we try to make purchases locally instead of importing, even if it may cost a bit more. I have great difficulty writing the last line as I have always strived for the best price. What I'm trying to learn is to step back a bit and take a look at the big picture. Are we helping the individual? Yes of course, but our quest is to transform a nation one child at a time. This can also be said about a region, a commune or neighborhood.

Suppose we need bikes for children to ride to school. We look to see if there is someone locally, in the city or commune, that sells the bikes rather than using our normal bike connection and importing them. This aids the local economy and builds relationships and favor with local governments. Another friend used to buy blankets and ship them into the villages in Africa. Now, instead he has helped locals to make the blankets and purchase from them thus aiding the economy of the village.

A popular thing is to bring gifts to Vietnam, often clothes or items for the kids of the country guests are from. A nice thought for sure, as kids like the idea it's from the US, but really is it made in the US? LOL, rarely. Most often things in the US are imported. I have tried to encourage guests and visitors to buy locally, helping the local economy.

Who Needs To Be A Hero?

Tet is the lunar new year in Asia and is a time where gifts are given to children and family members. They believe that how you enter the new year will bring you good luck or bad luck as the case may be. Families will go into debt painting their homes and buying new things. For poor families they are already in debt. Buying goodies for the kids is impossible.

For many years we would give Tet gifts to the poor children of the communities. I would proudly stand on the stage and hand baskets full of goodies, cookies, candies, and snacks to the poor children of the community. I remember looking back and seeing moms standing in the back of the room even though there were empty chairs and never would I see a father. Many photos would be shot of me and the poor children. Then it hit me, who needs to be the hero in this thing? The thought came from reading a book and I realized that we had it all backwards.

Our answer to this was to open a Tet Store. We talked to local businesses and had them loan us the snacks, dresses, clothes, jackets, stuffed animals and toys, all the things the kids and families like. We would set up a store in a local restaurant or some type of hall and charge ten cents on the dollar. We would invite the same families that we would have for the Tet Basket giveaway. They would be limited by certain amounts as to how much they could spend. If we learned that they didn't have even that much money, we would offer them an opportunity to come to the office and do some work, like dusting or cleaning windows, something simple. They could earn what they needed to have the amount so they could shop.

What transpired shocked me. All of sudden we had families engaged, fathers were coming often holding dresses or toys up saying, "Which one do you think she would like?" They would tell us, "We've never been able to buy things for our kids, but now we can!" Who needs to be the hero?

In the same way, we look to make the community leader or the government official the hero. We don't need our name on anything, although it is usually mentioned. We have the local community leader be the hero or the front person, we get to be in the background. What that has done is it's given us favor with the government and with the community leaders. They're happy to hear from us and to see us, because we lift them up, making them look good in their communities. So who needs to be the hero?

Government Should Be Honored

My parents fled the Soviet Union. In my home, communism was not a good word. In fact in the country I am from, communism is something to be feared. Vietnam is a communist nation. And though in many ways I don't agree with the government policies, I needed to learn and be reminded to honor the government and the laws. One thing that we were very fortunate with is even though many times we met government officials in formal settings, more often than not, also at informal spots. That is where we can build a relationship through friendships over coffee or dinners. I cannot emphasize enough of the importance and the favor that we've had with the government in Vietnam, and how it has helped us to grow to be effective.

Earlier I talked about who needs to be the hero. It's important that the government officials be the heroes in each of the areas we work in, to honor them and praise them whenever possible, to become friends and grow our relationships with them. Doing so has made the path for Giving It Back To Kids smoother, especially when we begin new programs or if we have problems.

Guests

Beware of a "Western" mind set, where others come to put out fires where there are no fires, or when there are fires, trying to put them out before learning where the base or source is. This is much like a novice with a fire extinguisher aiming at the top of the flames rather than the base. Often difficult conversations need to happen explaining things like culture and helping guests to recognize that sometimes the best thing is to say no or not at this time.

Learners Versus Servers

Sometimes the best way to serve is first by learning. Learning the people, the culture, and recognizing the real need rather than what may seem obvious to us, our mind set or the culture we are familiar with. These days I'm more careful about calling our trips vision trips. I prefer trips designed to inspire and educate those who come, to bring value rather than just build something. When I say bring value it means something that we will leave with the country.

Often people ask if it wouldn't be better if they just gave GIBTK the money rather than spend it on a trip? Sure, maybe in some cases this is true. But think with me, what value does an unconditional hug mean to an orphaned child in Vietnam?

The Value Of A Hug

I'm reminded of the story about my friends the Binkley's, who have worked in Zimbabwe for years. After my wife's memorial I had people over to the house. I was keeping very busy washing dishes and just staying out of the way and all conversations. I was doing anything to deflect the pain that I felt.

My friends Bruce and Camella had asked if they could bring a friend. He was a young man they knew as a child in an orphanage in Zimbabwe. They were at the far end of our great room, talking away as I tried to stay busy and detached, washing dishes. Then they came over and were standing next to the counter near me and I overheard the young man say, "Mr. Bruce I never knew what was in the boxes you brought, I just wanted a hug from you!" Typing this has brought a flood of emotion to me and again I'm fighting back tears.

I turned off the water and said, "excuse me for interrupting" and asked the young man would he please repeat what he just said. He said, "Sure, when I was living in the orphanage Mr. Bruce would bring boxes of things, as did so many other people. I never knew what was in the boxes, nor did I care. When Mr. Bruce came I would position myself in such a way that after he was done hugging all the other kids, I knew he would have to pass by me and I would get my hug." He went on to share that he learned the value of unconditional loving and safe touch, the value of a hug! He continued to explain that when other babies or young children would cry in the orphanage he would go and just hug them, hold them and sing songs to them. He would share his love with them. He went on to say that he now lives in the US, works at a Church as a worship director, and has written several scores for popular TV shows in the US.

So what value does a hug give us? The present of being there, not coming to fix a roof, a need, or "to put out fires." Just being there brings value. Of course sometimes there are days of real immediate needs, but I always have to weigh those with the facts, as well as the local circumstances. Also, would it be cheaper or better for me to just hire somebody to fix things?

With guests, I ask what are your gifts or talents? What do you know? How could you be a gift of yourself and talents? Are you a trainer, a business person, someone that can teach entrepreneurship or self-esteem? Or perhaps you can just hang out with the kids. I know through our friendship program we have connected our kids in Vietnam with others in the US, just being friends. We don't charge anything for it. It's about building relationships. A child in Southeast Asia or young adult can say I have a friend that stays in touch with me or came to visit me from 8000 miles away. Never underestimate the value of a person, thinking not what they can do, but who they are.

Ask Questions

One way I have found to engage and validate others' is to ask questions. The key here is we need to be vigilant about truly listening to their answers. As I spoke about earlier, listening is really an art. At least for me it is very challenging. I find myself saying to myself, get to the point! Or I'm getting ready to answer them because I already know or think I know, what they're getting ready to ask. Or I'm waiting for there to be a break in their conversation so I could talk and I'm preparing what I could say.

Some of the best minds, guys I've talked to over the years, are great question askers. They get me to thinking and pondering thoughts, looking for deeper answers. Another thing about asking questions, it's often you can help someone to find the answer to the dilemmas themselves, which is always a good thing. More often than not when we're faced with dilemmas, we already know the answer of what we should do. Not always true, but very often. I like question askers who make me think. Often when I sit with one of these men I come up with new thoughts, ideas, or programs and ways to engage others. Asking questions does not come naturally to me. I remind myself going into a meeting to ask questions.

As A Leader Be A Visionary!

This means to know where we are personally and organizationally. Also, to know where we're headed. Regularly and always cast vision.

I heard my pastor once teach that all vision leaks. He held up a large cup and filled it with water. The thing was, that the cup had holes in it. The water drained out. He had to keep refilling the cup. He said, "So it is with vision. It leaks and it must be refilled in those we lead."

Staying Connected

I often have used this example with the GIBTK team. Imagine a flower growing in soil. Others see the flower and say it is beautiful and each day it opens up revealing even more of its beauty. It continues opening up one day after the next, getting more and more beautiful. It stays beautiful as long as it's connected to the soil. I then cut the flower off and handed it to one of the staff. I ask them if it's still beautiful, right? But let's look at this in a few days. It will start to wither and die.

This is much the same way as our organization. We must stay in contact with those we help. We must stay in contact with those who support us. They are the "soil". We must be in a relationship. Yes being in relationships is time-consuming and often inconvenient. However, it will keep the flower blooming.

I feel too often other organizations that were there when we first started GIBTK, stalled out. They seem to never catch up to what's going on today and never upgraded their services. Their printed materials remained the same, eye catching to a former time. Their team training was minimal. Yes, they were big organizations, but they didn't continue to grow. And when we're not growing, decay begins to set in. Climate and culture change in the countries you're working in. The families you work with and the kid's needs you work with change as well.

It was not too many years ago that texting became the "new" thing. I remember being puzzled and confused. Even telling others why would I ever text? Well today I text a lot. It's even an inexpensive way to communicate when I'm in the US with our team in SE Asia. Side note is I must be careful that my texts are clear and not up for misinterpretation. What about social media? When it first came around, I was totally dumbfounded. Today it is a vital way for us to communicate with donors, as well as ways for those wanting to help or needing help. If the organization doesn't continue to change and adapt it will become lost history. Others will ask, "What ever happened to....?"

Don't Get The Cart Before The Horse

There's been many times that I see what's ahead for Giving It Back To Kids and with my impulsiveness, I start going there. It's a great place to use pause, LOL. As a visionary we are to see ahead, but we need to think about timing and preparation.

Even today there is a new country I'm looking and wondering about and asking God about our way to get involved. Our team has already been on an exploratory trip, but what's the next step? When is the correct time? I am aware that too often there might not be the "right time" and use that as an excuse to put it off. So let me rephrase it by saying, "When it is God's time!" I heard John Maxwell say, "A visionary sees where we're headed, the destination, and we need to gather navigators to show us the direction of how to get there."

Ego- Edging God Out

Of myself I am nothing. This is something that is clear in my life. Coming from the background I did; drug addiction, alcoholism, little education and leading the organization I get to lead, well quite honestly it is way bigger than me. Yet there are times that I, for lack of a better way to say it, say to myself, "Hey, look at the organization you built." Honestly, if left to my own ways and thinking, I'm a mess. There are so many instances that reflect that the living God called me to do this. Irrefutable evidence of a living God! Yes I've got wonderful people around me, but to be honest where did they come from? My marketing? LOL.

In the early days I remember asking close friends that if and when they see my ego starting to bloom, to please make me aware. I like the acronym for ego, which is Edging God Out. That's where I get into trouble, when I use my good ideas instead of God's ideas or if I get so focused on what I want to get done, that I'm stepping over people that are already hurting. I recently saw it put this way— God's writing the book. I better give Him back the pen.

Another of my woodshed experiences so to speak, was when we had a renowned leader coming to Vietnam. Besides leading a mega church, he was a key leader in the business communities around the world. He was a counsel to two presidents that I know of. His list of importance goes on and on.

One day his staff contacted me and said he wanted to come to Vietnam and wanted to know if our organization was interested in helping facilitate and arrange the trip. Of course we were interested. We had helped host several conferences for the association he led over the past few years. We worked using his training and his experience. We began the whole process of getting visas and making arrangements.

I was then contacted again and told that his wife had a friend whose husband worked in Vietnam and he wanted to speak to me. The man had an extensive education with many titles and letters after his name. I was humbled to speak to such a man of importance. He felt that the leader I'm speaking of, should come in under a special type of visa and that he would arrange for meetings with the vice president of Vietnam. Honestly I was dwarfed, I just shrunk into saying "Oh, OK if you think that that's what should be done." However I had this feeling inside of me that was different. My plans were to have this key leader meet with my friends, the government officials that were all Central Committee members, mid-level to higher. He would come as a friend, to see if there's anything his organization could do to help with leadership development.

Instead I backed off, gave way to the one who was 'more qualified'. What happened is the friend was unable to get the special visa, so they used the visa I had provided. There was no meeting with the vice president. There was great concern by the Vietnamese government in that they thought he was coming in to speak on human rights and religious freedoms. That was not the case as he was coming to see how he might be able to serve and train leadership. The whole event went well, but I was told by government friends to stay away. That I shouldn't be associated with that because it might cause problems for our organization in the future.

Not only did I miss the opportunity to spend a few days with this world renowned leader, but I truly believe that key appointments were missed because I stepped back. I was scared by the man with many titles. I felt as though God took me out to the woodshed and said, "If you're going to lead, lead, if not get out of the way." I say all this and that the key lesson is when you have been called you best go with it!

Fear

There's so many acronyms for fear and discussions on fear. Things like fear knocked on the door and faith answered and there was no one there... Or

F ace
E everything
A and
R ecover

Often fear is put in as something to be avoided or to fight against. And this is true. But fear can be a good thing. It keeps us from doing stupid or dangerous things. Or at least some of us. This might ruffle a few feathers. I often hear people say fear and faith cannot exist in the same place or same time. The contrarian in me says, yeah but. I've never jumped out of an airplane, but my guess is that at least the first time, there is fear mixed in with faith. Fear of jumping out of a perfectly good airplane and falling to the ground and faith that the parachute will open and glide safely to ground. I argue faith and fear often coexist.

In leading GIBTK, fear happens. Sure in the beginning I don't remember feeling a lot of fear. It was small and manageable or at least I thought it was. As I said previously, I knew a handful of people that would most likely support it the first year. Through my contacts I figured we could make a good three-year run. The truth is none of that handful ever gave anything the first year and it wasn't until after the third year that we began to grow. But as we grew and initiated new programs, fear and faith has and still does exist.

Every year when I see the new projected budget there is fear. When we move into a new country and we've just begun work in our third country, there is fear. But there's also faith that if it be God, it will be done. Just last night we were having dinner with volunteers at my home. And jokingly, but truthfully, we were laughing that maybe one of the reasons God chose me to lead this organization is that I know of myself I could not do it. That I needed to have faith in a God to make it happen.

I remember many times thinking if it doesn't happen, oh well I get to stay home more and go fishing. I say that very bravely, but the truth is my heart would be broken. I am so glad that we keep pushing into the areas that we are afraid of, poking at subjects that might not be so common or popular because I'm seeing lives changed. Changed for generations to come. So what's the fear that's stopping you from doing something you're called to? Maybe it's something in your home, family, a neighbor or maybe it's transforming your city or a nation! Better to try than wonder if?

Good Idea or God's Idea?

So often "I" come up with good ideas, others can come up with great ideas. We need to do the best possible, strive and be vigilant to distinguish between good ideas and God ideas. This is where having trusted friends, whom we are in a relationship with, can help us to distinguish if it's God's idea or not. Then we need to learn to move in God's time. This is a tough one for me and for many of my friends. Being a visionary, as a leader I see where to go, a new country or new program, a new commune. But it's important to know if it is God's timing or not yet. Or there are times that it is just a good idea and not something that needs to be done by us or at least not at this time. I can't say this enough, what's crucial is that we have those we are in a relationship with, that are current with us. We need friends we can talk with and listen to their opinions. Seek wise counsel always. Once we've done that, we can make a better decision, hopefully the right decision.

Servant leadership is a key in a good healthy leadership model. I have a tendency once I see the vision to go charging, pulling people along with me or maybe better said trying to pull people, wondering why they don't get it. Why won't they make the follow up calls? Why won't they do as we spoke and agreed upon in the last training? Another way to say it, or I should think it, is why don't I do what I ask others to do. I feel that a good leader models what he's asking others to do. I need to constantly remind myself to <u>lift</u> others up. Notice I didn't say pull up.

Progress Rather Than Perfection

All of our teams need correction from time to time. Always be sure to praise in public and correct in private. A little praise or an atta boy, or atta girl can and does go a long way! Those seeing their teammates praised often may think, hey I want to hear that about me and be influenced to do what their teammate does. So it's a win-win with just a little praise.

In the same way, a team member when corrected in private, out of the view of others, will usually appreciate that you took the time to sit with them in private and help lift and build them. Of course there will always be those who fight and resist any and all corrections. Oh well....maybe they will have a better experience in their next job?

We often can learn our biggest lesson from our failures. The key is to own our mistakes. Recognize them, or at least our part and try to learn from them. Remember it's progress rather than perfection. Clearly perfection is not something that is attainable for people like me and probably most of you. But I need to keep learning, keep progressing and yes so much as I hate to admit it, keep making mistakes.

Again, I often tell my team that if we are not making mistakes we are not trying anything new. Making mistakes is part of growth, of being on the cutting edge, looking to find answers for today's problems. I also tell them please don't make the same mistake over and over again let's learn from them. Let's grow from them, mature from them.

Example Of The Good Samaritan Teaching

I was in a men's meeting and Michael Tenpenny was speaking on the Good Samaritan story from the Bible. There are several lessons to learn from this story. On this day, the following was the lesson he wanted to highlight. It's about two religious leaders. Each one of them walked past, even crossed the street, to avoid a man laying in the street who was bleeding. They kept going because they had to get to where they were going. They had a "mission" that best not be slowed down.

The first 80% of his talk was funny. He talked about sheep and how they're not the smartest of animals. The next 10% Mike began to meddle in my life. The last 10% I wanted to choke the life out of him. Ok maybe not really, but I saw myself and how I was much like the men who walked past the injured man. I saw that I too was so mission minded that I stepped over or maybe better said, through so many that needed my attention. I'd fly into Vietnam to help the kids and you best not get in my way or slow me down! No matter if it was at the airports, hotel or most importantly my staff. I was harsh and most likely rude.

My lesson was to be aware of all that I crossed paths with. Learn to be a listener to all. I am still learning this lesson as I try to remember to be kind to those I come across daily, maybe the checker or bagger at the market. Just a simple hello, how are you today makes a difference. It's amazing to see how often they will stop scanning, look up and say thank you. Or maybe it's the difficult (ok I'm using nice words to describe) neighbor. How about saying hello or maybe an act of kindness to those who might not be so deserving? Honestly I can't say I've learned this lesson, but surely am becoming more and more aware.

Another example I try to keep in mind about the danger of being so mission minded, is that I can cause damage along the way. I have spent a lot of time on boats, specifically fishing boats. I often have left Newport Harbor Bay and have seen boats cause damage. In the Harbor there is a 5 mile an hour speed limit. There are times I see boats heading to Catalina Island, which is a popular destination. Often boats will kick up their speed, especially as they approach the mouth of the harbor. The island is their destination and can often be seen on the horizon.

The problem lies in that there are still homes along the harbor with boats tied to their docks. The captains seeing their destination, (may I say leaders) don't notice the wake their ship or boat is making at this higher speed and so often can tear boats off their moorings, damaging the moored boats and docks. We need to be mindful as leaders of the wakes we create, especially as we kick up our speed to fulfill our vision or destination.

I also remember in the early years walking on the beach where I used to spend a lot of time and still do, seeking God and thanking and praying about Giving It Back To kids. This one particular morning I was particularly excited and was just about shouting out loud to God about protecting the kids in Vietnam, that they might fulfill their destiny in God. I was looking for new ways to make a difference in their lives and then...it was like I had this quiet voice inside of me, a gentle whisper, maybe a God whisper? I heard,

"What about the two kids you have at home? What about the wife you have at home?" I realized one more time I was so mission minded, so into getting things done in Southeast Asia, I was forgetting to take care of the first things and that was my own family.

Sadness and Depression Are Real

You are what you eat. What do I fill myself with? At the writing of this we are going through a Pandemic with the Covid-19 virus. Where I live we've been quarantined for over 7 weeks. The only time we are to be outside is for essential things. Most businesses are closed unless considered essential. My high point is having to go to the market and try to find some food. Toilet paper is a rare find! Many of the shelves are empty.

With my type of character I like to keep moving and to have things on schedule and plans. At this point for me to travel to Vietnam it's a two week quarantine in a Vietnamese military camp and probably the same coming back, only in a US camp. So travel is out. Depression can be real. All through the years of Giving It Back To Kids there have been many times that I wanted to quit, that I was depressed, sad or lonely.

I heard a speaker mention the other day that his mentor had told him that in leadership to expect a crisis about every 10 years. Thinking back there was the 2001 terrorist bombings. In 2010 we had the financial crisis and now this Pandemic in 2020. What I have to do or what has worked for me, is to be very careful what I put into my mind and spirit. Even when there is not a major crisis in the world or around me, I have to be aware- much like the popular saying, "You are what you eat."

What I put into my mind and into my spirit is what I begin to think and feel. It's been important to me when I watch TV to try to look for things that make me laugh out loud. Even though there's a quarantine and the gyms are closed, I've been getting out making myself walk, boring but walking. For me I have to double down on my spiritual side. In all honesty, even in this challenging time I've learned to reach out to people. I answer phone calls and I make phone calls. I do the opposite of what my mind tells me to do once again, contrary actions.

EPILOGUE

Thank you for picking up this book and getting this far. I hope in some way, somehow, there has been a principle or story you can use right away, or perhaps it reinforces something you already believe, maybe a confirmation. My hope and prayer is that it may fan a spark already in your hearts and minds and that maybe you'll realize that if that uneducated pizza guy that fished a lot and had a very checkered past can do it, maybe I can too!

Perhaps some of the stories or principles you liked a bit more than others. Take what you could use, with the keyword being use. Others might be like the seeds of a watermelon or a piece of fruit. They might not be something you can eat or digest just now, but seeds are good things. They can be for the future and they too can produce fruit.

What are you going to do with this stuff you just learned? You might say, "Oh yes I am willing, oh man I really want this." However, as I mentioned earlier in this book, willingness without action is nothing but a fantasy.

Take a first step, find someone to serve under in faithful service. Maybe begin talking to others or knocking on doors. For me it's praying. But all that stuff, as important as it is and vital, means nothing unless I take the action.

There's an old Chinese proverb that goes something like this; "When is the best time to plant a tree? Five years ago. When's the next best time to plant a tree? NOW!"

If I may refer back to the story of the New Testament of the disciples in the boat when the storm came up and Jesus came walking out to them. Peter said, "If it's you let me come," but Peter had to get out of the boat and he had to take the first steps. And as I mentioned earlier in the book, what about the other eleven? They just sat and watched. I know it's not in scripture but I kind of believe that a couple of those guys may have been thinking, "should I ask," "should I try walking?" Maybe not, but don't be one of those afraid to get out of the boat if there's something on your heart you need to do. Plant the tree! Maybe it could be something as simple as being of service to a neighbor or whoever crosses your path during the day.

If you've gotten this far in the book I've got to believe there's something on your heart. Something that may be a gentle "whisper" or perhaps a "nagging" tug. Much like Peter getting out of the boat, he took steps. I'm reminded of something Dr. Cole often said, "despise not the day of small beginnings." We often never will know what ripples a small gesture or a small action can do or begin.

At the end of the book I am including my contact information, my personal cell phone number, my office number, as well as my email. If you need someone to talk to, contact me. Let's see what it takes to get you out of the boat.

Robert Kalatschan
www.givingitbacktokids.org
Office 714-593-9200
Mobile 714-423-3515
robert@givingitbacktokids.org

Made in the USA
Las Vegas, NV
01 October 2022

56348005R00085